Mark Knego

SNAKES
OF
KAMPUCHEA

a trilogy of plays about Cambodia

EX T
PRESS
SAN FRANCISCO

Snakes of Kampuchea
Copyright © 1991, 1993, 1994, 2011 by Mark Knego
All rights reserved

Published by EXIT PRESS
Assistance for this publication was provided by the
Kenneth R. Rainin Foundation
Cover Buddha sculpture by Phy Hem, 1989
Back cover photos by Laurie Gallant
Book design by Richard Livingston

First Edition: May 2011

The author can be contacted at knegoart@aol.com

For additional information about EXIT PRESS, go to
www.theexit.org.

ISBN: 978-0-9843964-1-2

EXIT PRESS
156 Eddy Street
San Francisco, CA 94102-2708
mail@theexit.org

Contents

Introduction

The city of San Francisco, a lovely inhabitation, is nestled comfortably on a peninsula. This peninsula lies on the west coast of the United States in California. San Francisco resides at a latitude of 37 degrees 37 minutes North and a longitude of 122 degrees 26 minutes West. It's time zone is -7 compared to Greenwich Mean Time. It is the gateway to Asia. In it's time, the city and state have been known as many things. Gold Mountain, The Promised Land, Rainbow City; and, as some would have it, even the Golden Road to Unlimited Devotion.

It is also known as home.

The city glitters in late afternoon sunlight on a spring afternoon, and ever-present evening fog soothes the conflicted. Downtown, uptown, it's all right here. And in the center of the city lies a neighborhood known as the Tenderloin, banked between Union Square, the major retail zone, and the Civic Center, the seat of the powers that be and those powers that have been.

In the past, the Tenderloin gleamed as it bopped to a post-war be-bop beat, as the hip and the hep and the happening, the white and the black and the asian frequented great jazz clubs to relish that current sound. It was glamorous.

But today this Tenderloin is bruised. Life's been rough. The Tenderloin is a black eye caterwauling down the street at 8am yet still deftly weaving around bright, day-glo backpack schoolchildren.

It's a multi-cultural neighborhood. One of the sharper facets of this tarnished emerald is the Southeast Asian refugee community.

Lao, Vietnamese and Cambodian families cram into residential apartment buildings. They all escaped from the Vietnam War (known as "the American War", to some) and it's spillovers; and settled into this country as part of the United Nations' Third Country Resettlement Program.

I found this out when I received a California Arts Council

Artist-in-Residence grant in 1987, and, being sponsored by SOMAR, South of Market Art Resources, which is housed at the South of Market Cultural Center, I began teaching art to these refugees at North of Market Senior Services on Turk Street near Leavenworth, as part of their Social Day Care Program. This was an art class; not an art therapy class. Initially we did masks in paper-mache, then moved on to collage.

Slowly I began to learn more about my students. Gradually, the class became an all Cambodian class. Generally these folks are agricultural workers, farmers, from Cambodia's northwestern Battambang province; and had survived the hell of the Pol Pot-Khmer Rouge auto-genocide of the late 1970s; managed to deal with years in scary refugee camps along the Thai border, generally at Site 2, Site B, Nong Chan or most notably Khao I Dang; and had harrowing, totally frightening experiences. Now they were living in the Tenderloin, which is, it assumedly goes without saying, another alien world for these folks. They had tales to tell. But nobody would listen.

In the art class, they found they could begin to tell their stories to the Americans.

I was moved by their experiences. I began incorporating their stories into my own artwork. At the time I was doing paper-mache sculptures. I started creating life-size animal figures in paper-mache collaged with scenes from the Southeast refugee experience.

And, surprisingly, the students, primarily ladies from their 40s to late 60s, stuck with the class. I never thought it would last beyond a year, because of the strangeness it must have encompassed for them. But the class was not a somber therapeutic chore, instead the classroom would ring with laughter as the ladies found a home away from home to meet others who shared their language, culture and experiences. I knew they were hooked when they started bringing me lunch(!). It was an experience for which I will always be so grateful.

About this time I had the fortune to meet Christina Augello of EXIT Theatre, who suggested that I write a play about this story, and EXIT would produce it. We did, and *Snakes of Kampuchea*, which portrays the Khmer Rouge takeover of Cambodia and the flight to the West, premiered in June, 1991. We decided that it would be a good idea to create a trilogy; thus, *Tual Kan's Journey* (1993), about a family's struggle to survive in the United States, and *Return to Angkor* (1994), which tells the story of a Cambodian woman's return to her homeland, rounded out The Cambodia Trilogy. I was very happy to have the opportunity to pursue this work.

Much of the background information for these plays obviously comes from my time spent with the Cambodian ladies, yet I was also fortunate to interview Cambodian natives Miss Sotie Ken, Miss Julie Tang and Mrs. Tuan Kan for additional material, and I would like to thank them wholeheartedly for their input.

A note about style. These are symbolic dramas. My theater work has always been very visual, with masks, body costumes, sculptural pieces, inherently dramatic sound cues, expressionistic lighting and other tools as I try to reach a kind of total theater - where every technical element can supplement the script, and not simply disappear into the background, as a slave to the script.

I believe there is more to theater than words and I believe in theatricality, using the techniques of the stage obviously, not hiding them behind a scrim.

The acting style, in my estimation, is best if naturalistic; and with the visual-audial background, the effect is ultimately surreal. I believe this style fits this theme for two reasons. One, it helps portray the extremeness of the experience; secondly, traditional Cambodian culture, which my student-clients definitely came from, is very folkloric, where animist beliefs and practices and other non-Western viewpoints are common. So spirits and masks and costumes are perfectly appropriate.

One note about a piece of vocabulary from "Return to Angkor". In this piece the locals refer to the Khmer Rouge as "black dog soldiers" because "they treated us like dogs and dressed in black".

I would like to thank the California Arts Council and South of Market Art Resources for sponsoring this project, and also sincerely thank, in deep gratitude, the staff at North of Market Senior Services; Vera Haile, Gay Kaplan, Jason Bernardi and Sopath Pak. I would also like to thank Silen Nhok, and my Cambodian friend Nara Tan.

Great thanks also goes to EXIT Theatre, and especially to

Christina Augello and Richard Livingston. Needless to say, you are terrific producers, an essential part of the Bay Area theater scene, and also great travel partners! I am so grateful for all that you have done for me, and also for so many others.

Lastly, I must thank the women and men who participated in my class, the Cambodia Contemporary Arts Project. Clearly, none of this would have happened without you. I have no words to describe my feelings and thoughts for you. I feel as if I had been touched by an angel during those years.

I hope you and your families are well.

Thank you for letting me take your class.

Mrs. Sith Ouch
Mrs. Rath Kan
Mrs. Luk Kan
Mrs. Pum Seing Aing
Mrs. Soeun Iv
Mrs. Tho Soh Iv
Mrs. Leang Ngin
Mrs. Phy Hem
Mr. Hun Rath
Mr. Chea San
and
Miss Ky Iv

Please enjoy the plays.

Mark Knego
May 2011

SNAKES OF KAMPUCHEA

a symbolic drama about
Cambodia and the Khmer Rouge

Snakes of Kampuchea

Snakes of Kampuchea premiered on June 20, 1991 at EXIT Theatre in San Francisco, California. The play was directed by the author, who also designed and built the masks. The play was produced by EXIT Theatre, with the following original cast and crew:

COMRADE DIN	Montgomery Hom
COMRADE TRAN	Diana Weng
COMRADE CHAN	Joseph Hong
KAN	Janis Chow *
VILLAGE DOCTOR	Frank Young
SONEE	Timothy Franklin
SOMALIA	Corinne Chooey
SOTIE	Sotie Ken
FROG SPIRIT	Frank Young
SNAKE SPIRIT	Timothy Franklin
FISH SPIRIT	Corinne Chooey
NAGA CROCODILE SPIRIT	Timothy Franklin
WAR SLAVE	Frank Young

* Linda Nakamura replaced Janis Chow as KAN for the final two weeks of the run.

Sound and Light Design	Tony Avoid
Sound and Light Operator	Rick Garlinghouse
Cambodian Performance Interpreter	Sophath Pak
Photos	Laurie Gallant

Cast of Characters

COMRADE DIN, Khmer Rouge commander
COMRADE TRAN, female Khmer Rouge soldier
COMRADE CHAN, male Khmer Rouge soldier
KAN, a woman in the village

VILLAGE DOCTOR
SONEE, a young man in the village
SOMALIA, a girl in the village
SOTIE, a Cambodian farmer
FROG SPIRIT, SNAKE SPIRIT, FISH SPIRIT, NAGA
CROCODILE SPIRIT, actors in full head animal masks
WAR SLAVE, refugee

Stage Set

Empty; black, brown, green and dark colors on floors and walls.

Time and place

A small village in Cambodia in the early 1970s. Despite the delineation of scenes in the script, action should flow seamlessly throughout the piece, along with the sound and lights.

Note

** denotes lines delivered in Cambodian

Scene One

Stage dark. A small light appears onstage. It comes out of a box that COMRADE DIN is holding. The light comes out of the box as he opens the lid. He looks forward toward the audience as small snakes slither out of the box. Sound of a snake rattle. COMRADE DIN closes the lid of the box. COMRADE DIN exits.

Sound - jungle sounds.
Lights up.
5 seconds no movement.
SOMALIA runs across stage.
5 seconds no movement.

SONEE follows her across stage.

SONEE Come back, come back! **

SOTIE enters, carrying a shoulderboard with a cassette player playing Cambodian folk music suspended from the board, smoking a large, handrolled cigar. She sits, places a wrapped banana leaf on the ground, opens it and eats rice and fish paste meal from the leaf as the cassette player continues to play.

SOMALIA runs across stage followed by SONEE.

SOTIE Watch out you fools, you stepped in my rice! **

SOMALIA, crossing from one direction, SONEE from the other, tackles her and they collapse on the ground laughing.

SONEE Now I've got you! **

SOMALIA Help me somebody! **

SOTIE You idiot, I thought you went to the field! **

SONEE Oh sister, I did go to the field! **

SONEE tickles girl, laughs.

SOTIE Yeah, yeah, OK.

SONEE So will you dance your dance again for us, sister?

SONEE tickles her again.

SOMALIA Yes, yes!

KAN enters.

KAN Are we working on the rice harvest today, or what?

SONEE Or what!

> *KAN exits.*

SONEE Sister, how are you, will you give me some rice?

SOTIE Sure.

SONEE Thanks!

> *All three eat for a few seconds.*

Ah, the village is the best. I will never move to the city.

SOTIE You should go to school.

SONEE I don't need to go to school. I need sister to dance for us!

> *SONEE tickles SOMALIA. He changes cassette to*
> *Cambodian folk dance music. SOMALIA performs basic*
> *Cambodian dance for their obvious pleasure.*
> *KAN enters with rice threshing tools.*

KAN Young man, let's get some work done here.

SONEE Sure, sure.

> *They thresh rice for five to eight seconds.*

KAN So did you actually get out to the fields, or did you spend all day chasing your neighbor?

SONEE Yes, I got out to the fields.

KAN We need to harvest it real fast and get to the market early to get a good spot.

SONEE Yes, yes, I know.

KAN If you're not going to school, you need to do something.

SONEE I am doing something. We always have enough to eat. We never worry about what's next.

KAN All you want to do is play like a little boy.

SONEE Cambodia has enough rice. Sihanouk says we are the best country in Asia. Of course I want to relax.

>   *Pause.*

KAN Uncle Seng came back from the city today.

SONEE Oh?

KAN He says that war is getting bigger.

SOTIE What war?

KAN I'm not sure. It's near Vietnam - and the north.

SOTIE Hmm. I never heard about it. I'm sure there's nothing to worry about.

SONEE Sssshh! Look!

>   *SONEE turns off cassette player. A FROG SPIRIT enters.*
>   *SONEE takes small fish from pocket, attaches it to string,*
>   *and tosses it to FROG SPIRIT. As FROG moves toward*
>   *fish, he pulls on string, and FROG follows it, until it arrives*
>   *center stage. SONEE removes fish, and feeds it to frog.*
>   *FROG swallows fish, then exits.*

SONEE Did you see that!

KAN You are very good with the frog!

> *SOMALIA giggles and SONEE tickles her. KAN continues to thresh rice. A sound is heard off in the distance. As it becomes louder, they notice it, and surprised, run downstage center looking up in the sky. Sound is deafening, passing over and fading out.*

SONEE An airplane.

SOTIE I've never seen one before.

> *Greyout.*

Scene Two

> *6 months later. Lights up. KAN, SONEE, SOTIE sitting downstage. Rice pot, clothes nearly. SOMALIA runs in out of breath.*

SONEE Are they here yet?

SOMALIA They're entering the village from the south side.

SONEE Are the near Chea's house?

SOMALIA Past it. Closer. They will be here any moment.

SONEE What do they look like?

KAN How many are there?

SOMALIA There are a few of them...but they don't act like regular soldiers.

KAN What do you mean?

SOMALIA They are very dirty. They do not march together like I've seen the Lon Nol solders. They are dressed in black pajamas. And they...

KAN Yes?

SOMALIA They are very young.

> *SOMALIA exits.*

KAN I am very worried.

SONEE Don't worry. I'm sure they're very tired from the fighting. They will not hurt us.

SOTIE They say the Khmer Rouge do not even steal a grain of rice.

KAN How do you know?

SOTIE Somebody said.

SONEE I heard it too.

SOTIE Anyway, anything will be better than war. Lon Nol was a terrible government. I'm glad the war's over for us.

SONEE I agree completely. Now that it's over, we will have peace. I am so happy, I cannot tell you! No more fighting, no more hiding, no more corrupt soldiers, kidnapping us for ransom. Lon Nol was a corrupt dictator, he didn't know how to run the country, he encouraged corruption and himself was the biggest thief of all. I spit on his grave!

> *SONEE spits.*

SOTIE I don't know much about communism, but they say that everybody is equal, especially the peasants. That's what the Viet Cong fight for. We are the peasants, so we can be equal too!

SONEE I've put out a white sheet at my house to greet them with surrender. There is white all over the village. It's so beautiful! Some people are getting rice for them. Do we have rice?

SOTIE Yes, yes, some rice!

KAN I still worry.

SONEE Why?

KAN My husband met the oracle last night. He said to walk out of the village, leave his family and everything behind or great harm would come to him.

SOTIE That's crazy. How could he leave you behind like that? That is crazy advice. I always thought that old man was crazy.

SONEE Don't worry Kan.

DOCTOR enters.

KAN Have you heard?

DOCTOR Yes, of course.

SOMALIA enters.

SOMALIA They are searching all the houses.

SOTIE I wonder why.

DOCTOR Probably looking for soldiers. Or guns.

SOTIE Nothing like that here.

DOCTOR Well at last this stinking war will be over. They will probably push on to Phnom Penh and drive the Lon Nol people out.

SOMALIA Here they are!

> *COMRADE TRAN, with AK-47 rifle, dressed in black pajamas, tire sandals and traditional Cambodian kramaa, enters meekly.*

ALL Hello.

> *Surprised, they stand, bow in sompeah, traditional Cambodian greeting.*

SONEE Welcome to our village of Bong Rae.

COMRADE TRAN Yes, comrade, thank you.

> *SONEE gestures for KAN to give her some rice.*
> *COMRADE TRAN sits and eats quickly. Others sit also.*

KAN *(As an aside to others, in a whisper)* She is a woman! There are women Khmer Rouge!

SOTIE Has there been much fighting?

COMRADE TRAN Yes. There was a big battle three days ago. We walked all night. I am so hungry and tired.

SOTIE Do you shoot the gun?

COMRADE TRAN *(slight smile)* Yes.

SOTIE Wow. *(pause)* What will happen? Is there a new government?

COMRADE TRAN The countryside will be re-organized into large collective farms. Everybody works together. That way we can recover from the war.

SOTIE What is a collective farm?

COMRADE TRAN Everybody works together on the same big plot of land. There is no individual ownership.

SOTIE Who's idea is that?

COMRADE TRAN Angka's idea.

SOTIE Who's Angka?

COMRADE TRAN *(pause)* I'm not sure. *(uneasy pause)* Thank you for the rice comrade. I have heard that the people of Bong Rae are very kind. This is proof. I wish I had something to give you. I wish you much luck sister. I think you will need it.

KAN Why?

COMRADE TRAN The crocodile cannot control the waters of the lake.

SOMALIA Here's another one!

> *COMRADE CHAN, dressed like COMRADE TRAN, with pistol, enters nervously. He sees rice bowl, sits and wolfs down rice voraciously.*

SOTIE *(soft voice)* My God, what a pig.

COMRADE CHAN Stand up.

SOTIE What?

COMRADE CHAN *(rising)* Stand up now!!!

> *ALL stand and COMRADE CHAN and COMRADE TRAN search them and exit.*

KAN They do not seem very Cambodian to me.

DOCTOR Do not worry. They do not even steal a grain of rice. They seem very disciplined.

> *COMRADE CHAN and COMRADE TRAN enter.*

COMRADE CHAN and COMRADE TRAN Welcome to Comrade Din, commander in chief of this village of Democratic Kampuchea!

> *COMRADE DIN enters. ALL sompeah to COMRADE DIN.*

COMRADE DIN Good. Who is the chief here?

SONEE I am.

COMRADE DIN Good. At this point, I am reclaiming your authority in the name of the peoples of Democratic Kampuchea.

SONEE Sir?

COMRADE DIN Don't call me sir. Call me comrade. We are all equal here in Democratic Kampuchea.

SONEE Yes, "comrade."

COMRADE DIN You are all now part of the liberated zone. I cannot express to you how exciting this is for Kampuchea. We are here to completely restructure society. We call this year zero. Everything that was before -- laws, schools, government, temples, religion -- are no more. All that is replaced by Angka.

SONEE What is Angka?

COMRADE DIN Angka is the party.

SONEE What is the party?

COMRADE DIN The party is all of us together, one organization.

DOCTOR All of us, together?

COMRADE DIN Yes.

DOCTOR So we make all the decisions together?

COMRADE DIN Yes, but in order to speed up the offensive against nature and construct a wall to resist the foreign imperialists, the party leadership in it's benevolence makes the best decisions in your interest. Comrades, comrades. What do you need here in Bong Rae?

SONEE The fields are full of holes from the bombing. We need trucks and machines to fill them in.

COMRADE DIN And who is responsible for the bombing?

SONEE Uh...the Lon Nol government?

COMRADE DIN That's right! The capitalists in Phnom Penh. They are responsible. We have come to save you.

SONEE Thank you.

COMRADE DIN And do you know who is running Lon Nol? *(silence)* Foreigners. Lon Nol is full of foreigners.

DOCTOR What foreigners?

COMRADE DIN The French, for one. The capitalist French, with their "white wine", "brie" and "pate."

DOCTOR The French left twenty years ago. They built hospitals, schools, universities, dams and bridges. Sihanouk got our independence from them without firing a shot. There is no bad influence from them.

COMRADE DIN Their bad influence is morality. They are decadent. The foreigners are ruining the country. They are responsible for all our problems. We all must reorganize for the offensive against nature. But this will be difficult, comrades. Difficult because of impure foreign influence. The problem with Cambodia is that foreigners are running the country. They are part of the Lon Nol government. Because they don't understand us, they are destroying the nation. Americans. Vietnamese. Thai. They have no place in our new society. Am I correct?

Silence.

Yes, I am correct. We will purify the country of non-Khmer blood. Cambodia will prosper. Long live a prosperous Cambodia!

COMRADE CHAN and TRAN Long live a prosperous Cambodia!

COMRADE DIN So, in the coming days, we must reorganize the countryside into a collective farm.

DOCTOR We cannot farm our own fields?

COMRADE DIN Angka has decided to remove this impediment from you for your collective liberation.

DOCTOR Who is this Angka really?

COMRADE DIN Angka is the party. The peasants make up the party and the party is responsible for implementing the peasants' decisions. We consult all the people and make decisions based upon their wisdom. You are all now living in a state governed by peasants - a peasant state. You are the state, and the state is you. The party will look out for everything you need. You do not need to cook - Angka will cook for you. You do not need to watch your children - they can work too. We do not need an engineer - we can construct a dam with our bare hands. I do not need a doctor - I can cut with my own knife. Everything - and anything - is done in the name of the party. For the new Cambodia we must learn what you did in the old Cambodia, so we can assign the correct job for you. We will get paper and pencil and you will fill out a testimonial of your former occupations.

DOCTOR I'm sorry, but most of these people don't know how to read or write.

COMRADE DIN I see. What did you do for the Lon Nol government?

SONEE I don't understand.

COMRADE DIN Did you work for the government?

SONEE No ... I ... am a farmer.

COMRADE DIN Good. You are a "naht-kraw." *(smiles)*

SONEE Yes. *(smiles)*

COMRADE DIN Have you seen any foreigners?

SONEE Uh... I don't think so.

COMRADE DIN Good. You are a real Cambodian, then?

SONEE A real Cambodian.

COMRADE DIN Good! We need good Khmer people like you for our struggle, comrade. We will work to turn the fields into factories, and the factories into cities, so we won't have to grow rice by hand again! We won't need buffalo, or plow, or hoes and baskets. This whole valley will become a giant, shining city, yes, greater than the cities of China, greater than Peking, the greatest in Asia! Am I right, comrade? Is this our goal?

SONEE *(stunned)* Yes.

COMRADE DIN Good! *(applauds)* You are an example of the new Cambodia. I want you to do me a favor. Go to the next village and tell them of our revolution. Go. Go now.

> SONEE exits.

COMRADE DIN What about the girl? What did you do in the village?

DOCTOR Go ahead, don't be shy.

SOMALIA I... I worked in the fields for my uncle.

COMRADE DIN Planting rice? For your uncle?

SOMALIA Yes. And collecting food in the forest.

COMRADE DIN Do you go to school?

SOMALIA No.

COMRADE DIN If you work for your uncle, where are your parents?

SOMALIA My mother works with us and my...

COMRADE DIN And where is your mother now?

SOMALIA She is visiting my father in the city.

COMRADE DIN And what does he do in the city?

SOMALIA He works at the school.

COMRADE DIN At the Lycee?

SOMALIA Yes.

COMRADE DIN What does he do? Is he a teacher? A professor?

SOMALIA Something like that, I think.

DOCTOR He is in administration.

COMRADE DIN So he works for the government at a foreign school. He has been dirtied by foreign contact. He is a foreigner.

SOMALIA He's Cambodian. Sir.

Lights dim slightly.

COMRADE DIN Come, come.

> *COMRADE DIN gently takes SOMALIA by her wrist and pins her to a post. Then he pulls out a knife, not well seen by the audience. With his body partially blocking the audience's view, at a very close proximity, he slashes SOMALIA three times on the upper chest. She screams each time. The knife leaves easily visible blood streaks on her shirt as COMRADE DIN steps aside. SOMALIA falls to the ground unconscious, but is still breathing. COMRADE DIN slashes her leg.*

DOCTOR No. No! How could you!

> *Lights dim up to previous illumination. COMRADE DIN walks downstage slowly, brandishing knife. The he puts knife in its sheath.*

COMRADE DIN There is no room for impure foreigners in Democratic Kampuchea. What did you do for the Lon Nol government?

DOCTOR I did nothing for the Lon Nol government. I am the village doctor, sir!

COMRADE CHAN Call him comrade!

COMRADE DIN Are you a krou Khmer?

DOCTOR No, I am a Doctor.

COMRADE DIN We don't need "doctors."

DOCTOR I studied in Phnom Penh! I have an excellent education! I have been the village doctor for fifteen years!

COMRADE DIN Cambodia has been destroyed by foreigners and their doctors. We do not need Western medicine. *(touches knife)* I, will be the doctor. The Khmer who has worked with foreigners is dirty. Impure traitors will not be tolerated. We defeated them in our battlefield and we will defeat them in our revolution!

KAN Don't hurt my husband!

COMRADE DIN Your husband has worked with the foreigners. He is a scab, a parasite pus sac that must be cauterized. Long live the glorious, everlasting Kampuchean revolution!

COMRADES CHAN and TRAN Long live the glorious, everlasting, Kampuchean revolution!

COMRADE DIN Angka is like a pineapple. It has a thousand eyes and sees everything. Beware of the Khmer with the Vietnamese mind. Beware the city person. The American. The French. Long live our victory! Down with foreign imperialism! Long live the independent, peaceful, non-aligned, neutral, sovereign, everlasting benevolent Democratic Kampuchea!

COMRADES CHAN and TRAN Long live the independent, peaceful, non-aligned, neutral, sovereign, everlasting benevolent

Democratic Kampuchea!

COMRADE DIN Angka has a way of dealing with foreigners. With those who distrust the party. We are all equal in the eyes of the party. We can live together for the party or you can die together for the party. The snake is blind in the face of evil. Keep is no gain. Lose is no loss.

> *COMRADE DIN pushes the DOCTOR to the ground. A large SNAKE crawls in, crawls to the DOCTOR and crushes him to death. SNAKE then leaves.*

COMRADES DIN, CHAN and TRAN

> *In simple singing, while performing a dance miming work activities.*

Bright red blood
Over the cities and plains
Bright red blood
Over the cities and plains
Bright red blood
Over the cities and plains
Bright red blood
Of the Kampuchean revolution
We work in the day
We work all the night
For the revolution
To conquer the imperialists
Bright red blood
Of the Kampuchean revolution

Long live the Kampuchean revolution!
Long live the Kampucehan revolution!
Long live the Kampuchean revolution!

Blood avenges blood!
Blood avenges blood!
Blood avenges blood!

Blood avenges blood!

COMRADE DIN The fields are waiting comrades. Gather the war slaves for the harvest.

> *COMRADES DIN and CHAN exit. KAN runs to the body of the DOCTOR.*

COMRADE TRAN Plant a go tree, sister. The crocodile cannot control the waters of the lake.

> *COMRADE TRAN exits. KAN and SOTIE drag DOCTOR's body offstage.*

Scene Three

> *COMRADE CHAN enters with tire rim and rings it with metal bolt like bell. Then he drags SOMALIA, who is still alive, offstage. KAN, SONEE and SOTIE march in with hoes and begin digging.*

SONEE Never seen a government like this one.

SOTIE Huh?

SONEE Never seen a government like this one. Work all day, all night, for two bowls of rice water. I"m starving.

KAN I can't understand.

SONEE No fish, no meat, no medicine, no mail, no music, no nothing. Only Angka. What is Angka? Who is the Khmer Rouge leader, anyway?

KAN I still don't know.

SONEE And if you ask any questions... you disappear.

COMRADE CHAN walks across. Others quiet.
COMRADE CHAN exits.

SOTIE They took away the village mechanic last night. His whole family too.

KAN A body has truly passed away.

SOTIE It must be our karma.

SONEE The whole nation? The whole nation's karma is this bad?

SOTIE I think so, yes.

SONEE That is ridiculous. Use your mind. Karma cannot explain war. It is the result of politics.

KAN They know nothing of politics.

SONEE But they are communists!

KAN Have you ever heard them talk about "communists?"

SONEE We... well no, actually.

KAN They know nothing of politics. They just repeat the same slogans their commanders do. They don't even know what they are saying. They are stupid country boys, I tell you, and have been brainwashed! And the slogans, the uniforms... they are from China!

SONEE No, it's Vietnam. The Vietnamese trained them. They send our rice to Vietnam. I've seen truckloads of rice heading east.

KAN I don't know how they can do this to us. They are Cambodian too. They are evil. They are "sang-suk" people.

SONEE The crocodile has lost it's lake, truly. I remember seeing the white crocodile on the Mehkong three years ago. It was absolutely enormous.

KAN Really!

SONEE I didn't realize at the time what an omen it was. I didn't think things could get this bad. We bribed to survive under Lon Nol, now the Khmer Rouge are killing us!

> *COMRADE CHAN enters, holding pot of rice soup, bowls and spoons.*

COMRADE CHAN Lunch break, comrades.

> *KAN, SONEE and SOTIE sit. COMRADE CHAN puts utensils in front of war slaves, SOTIE pours thin soup into bowls and distributes them.*

SONEE Make it even this time. Not like yesterday.

> *The three drink soup quickly. They watch COMRADE CHAN eat large bowl of rice nearby.*

COMRADE CHAN What are you looking at? If you are finished, back to work. There is no room for parasites in Democratic Kampuchea!

> *COMRADE CHAN picks up pot and utensils and exits, others return to work.*

SONEE Maybe the Khmer Serei freedom fighters will rescue us.

SOTIE I hope so.

SONEE They are on the border. We can join them!

> *COMRADE CHAN peers in.*

KAN That's crazy. We can't even get past the garden without being caught. The garden is a joke anyway. Everybody is stealing from it so they won't starve, so there is almost nothing left. I myself do it. I get a big bag of corn, then crawl back to my hut.

SOTIE Me too. The whole work unit is out there at night. No wonder everybody's so sleepy.

KAN The only way out of the village is to die.

SONEE *(sees COMRADE CHAN)* Sssshhh!

COMRADE CHAN Angka is like a pineapple. It has a thousand eyes and sees everything. Comrade!

COMRADES DIN and TRAN enter.

COMRADE CHAN What is your name?

KAN Comrade Kan, comrade.

COMRADE CHAN Comrade Din, I heard Comrade Kan making counter-revolutionary statements against Angka.

COMRADE DIN Oh really?

COMRADE CHAN They were making... statements against Angka. Comrade Kan also said she steals from the community garden. At night.

COMRADE DIN I see. This is a major offense.

COMRADE CHAN Take her to Angka Leu. Take her to Angka Leu!

COMRADE DIN Stealing is forbidden. Only the foreigner steals.

COMRADE CHAN Let me kill her now!

COMRADE DIN I think she must visit Angka Leu first.

KAN No, comrade, please, I...

COMRADE DIN Perhaps you have other counter-revolutionary statements that Angka Leu needs to hear.

KAN Please, comrade, no.

COMRADE DIN Take her to Angka Leu!

COMRADE TRAN Wait!

COMRADE DIN Comrade?

COMRADE TRAN *(pause)* Perhaps Comrade Kan has made a mistake, this is clear. But I have watched her in her work unit. She works very hard, harder than the men. To lose her would be a loss.

COMRADE CHAN Keep is no gain, lose is no loss!

COMRADE TRAN In this case, comrade, I think that is not true. Comrade, I recommend that Comrade Kan not be punished and be forgiven for her counter-revolutionary statements.

COMRADE CHAN No!

COMRADE DIN Quiet! Do you take authority to make sure that this doesn't happen again?

COMRADE TRAN Yes, comrade.

COMRADE DIN Comrade Kan, what do you have to say?

KAN I apologize for making counter-revolutionary statements. I believe in Angka. I always try to do Angka's will, and I will not make counter-revolutionary statements again.

COMRADE DIN Good. If you do.... Angka will not be so lenient twice. Your hair is on your own head. Comrades, we must call a meeting.

> *COMRADES CHAN and TRAN usher the others to sit facing COMRADE DIN.*

COMRADE DIN It is time for Angka to issue new orders. The work on the canals has been progressing well, and the offensive against nature is productive. All praise to Angka! Long live our benevolent, glorious offensive against nature!

COMRADES CHAN and TRAN Long live our benevolent, glorious offensive against nature!

COMRADE DIN Angka has a new task for you. Now we must construct a dam to the northeast. With the dam and canals that we have already built, we can harvest three rice crops a year. The new dam offensive will begin tomorrow.

> *Pause.*

The wheel of history is turning, comrades. Whoever falls off, will be crushed. Time for sleep. We march to the new dam site in two days. Jay-oh Kampuchea!

COMRADES CHAN and TRAN Jay-oh Kampuchea!

COMRADE DIN Jay-oh Kampuchea!

COMRADES CHAN and TRAN Jay-oh Kampuchea!

> *COMRADES DIN and CHAN exit.*

KAN Comrade, you saved my life. How can I ever repay you?

COMRADE TRAN Plant a go tree, sister. "Dam doeum go." It has arrived, that which we could never name. The gods have made a terrible mistake.

> *COMRADE TRAN exits. KAN, SOTIE prepare to sleep in separate areas. SONEE scurries off surreptitiously. Lights and sound dim. Lights moody nighttime scene.*

Scene Four

> *Sound of frogs croaking.*

> *COMRADE TRAN enters holding a box. She moves stealthily toward the sleeping SOTIE. She opens her box, and light pours from the inside. She pulls three frogs from the box and places them around the sleeping SOTIE in a ritualized way. A large FROG enters.*

> *Sound of frogs and rainfall.*

> *COMRADE TRAN moves to the sleeping KAN. The FROG crouches over SOTIE in a protective position. COMRADE TRAN pulls a red fish from the light box and places it on the sleeping KAN. A FISH enters. COMRADE TRAN exits. The FISH kneels over the sleeping KAN in a protective position.*

> *A SNAKE enters, moves menacingly around SOTIE, then around KAN, then exits. Lights gently fade out. Sound cross-fades to jungle sound.*

Scene Five

> *Lights gently come up. SONEE and SOMALIA, seemingly exhausted and ill, sitting looking directly at the audience. COMRADES DIN, CHAN and TRAN are looking at the*

others.

COMRADE DIN We have called this meeting to let you, the peoples of Democratic Kampuchea, freely speak your minds about what concerns you. Long live the Kampuchean revolution!

ALL Long live the Kampuchean revolution.

COMRADE DIN The peasants make up the bulk of the party, and the party is responsible to carry out the wishes of the peasants. So would anybody like to use this opportunity to speak their mind?

Uneasy silence.

Surely someone must have an opinion.

SONEE *(stands)* I wish to thank the comrades for this opportunity to speak. *(hesitates)* You say that we are all equal in the peasant state. I see that we work very hard, and are given only two bowls of watery rice soup a day, while you soldiers do not work and eat much fish, pig and beef. How is this equal in a peasant state?

Agitation among the others.

COMRADE DIN Comrade, we are all equal. Surely you must be blind not to see this.

SONEE We are starving while you eat!

COMRADE DIN Comrade, please be reasonable. There are many different jobs to be filled in our revolution. Now some of these jobs are actually more difficult than others. Now the job of the soldiers is actually more difficult than the jobs of the workers. The soldiers of the Khmer Rouge are protecting you from destructive foreign influences. To do this they must be very alert. This is very difficult, more difficult than digging, and thus deserves a bigger ration.

SONEE You can't tell me that watching people with guns is more difficult than digging fourteen hours a day!

COMRADE DIN It is very difficult to watch for and spot traitors. There are traitors here amongst you, and they are very difficult to root out.

SONEE It is still not equal. I was poor under Lon Nol, but I was not hungry. Now I am poor and hungry.

COMRADE DIN We are all hungry. We all must share.

SONEE Then give me your rice! We see you eating rice, pig and fish, while we suck on insects and leaves!

COMRADE DIN Exactly! You traitors are stealing from the community garden at night. I completely agree with you! Do you think we do not know this? You deserve a low ration because you are stealing.

SONEE You are starving us!

COMRADE DIN We are all equal.

SONEE That is a lie!

COMRADE DIN Comrade, I suggest you stop your counter-revolutionary statements, or I will not be responsible for your safety!

COMRADE TRAN Quiet! Comrades, this is out of control!

COMRADE DIN Comrade Tran! Your work crew is unravelling. I suggest you keep your comrades more under control. It is for your own safety.

COMRADE TRAN Yes, comrade, it will not happen again.

COMRADE DIN Now I have something more disturbing to tell you. Recently, our enemies have dared to launch an attack against our borders. They are threatening the very existence of Democratic Kampuchea. Foreign aggressors are at our very throats.

SONEE The Khmer Serei!

SOMALIA The freedom fighters.

COMRADE DIN So beware of traitors. They are in our midst.

> *COMRADE DIN glares at SOMALIA.*

If you hear a traitor, do not speak with him, but report him to Angka. This is your duty to your motherland. Your sacred duty. Jay-oh Kampuchea!

ALL Jay-oh Kampuchea!

COMRADE DIN Jay-oh Kampuchea!

ALL Jay-oh Kampuchea!

COMRADE DIN Jay-oh Kampuchea!

ALL Jay-oh Kampuchea!

> *COMRADES DIN, CHAN and TRAN exit. SONEE sleeps on the ground. SOMALIA exits, limping. Lights dim to night scene. Sounds become cicadas chirping.*

Scene Six

> *COMRADES DIN and CHAN enter. COMRADE DIN carries box from first scene and a liquor bottle; COMRADE CHAN a bowl of rice. They are excited.*

COMRADE CHAN *(kicking SONEE)* Wake up, comrade!

SONEE Is it work already?

COMRADE DIN No, we have come for a visit, to have a meeting!

COMRADE CHAN Does he want to meet with Angka Leu?

COMRADE DIN Of course he does! But now Angka Leu has come to meet him!

SONEE What do you want?

COMRADE CHAN We are here to thank you for giving us this opportunity to speak, comrade. We are all equal, and you are hungry, right?

SONEE Well, actually, I am not that hungry right now.

COMRADE DIN Right, you are stealing from the community garden!

> *COMRADE CHAN gives SONEE huge bowl of rice and fish.*

COMRADE CHAN Have you ever seen such rice and fish, comrade? Look!

COMRADE DIN Here.

> *Passes bottle to COMRADE CHAN. He drinks from the bottle and passes it back to COMRADE DIN. They sit.*

COMRADE DIN Cambodia used to be so beautiful before the foreigners came. They are responsible for everything that is wrong in this country.

COMRADE DIN drinks, gives bottle back to COMRADE CHAN.

When the crops fail in the fields, it is because the Vietnamese have shamans to change the weather. When rice becomes too expensive, it is because the Americans can pay more. They have no rice, so they take ours! They say they are better than us, have bigger cities. It is a lie, we are the best! We are the best!

COMRADE CHAN That's right!

COMRADE DIN Cambodia is only for Cambodians. The Khmer. We are a superior race, yes. We built Angkor. What have the Thais done? The Lao? Nothing. The Vietnamese live a low life. They are a bacterial scum. They are like dogs... fucking. The Thai are traitors, and not to be trusted, because they work with the French. And they all work for the Americans, a very corrupt people. They steal Cambodian babies and take them back to their homeland to raise them.

COMRADE CHAN The Khmer with a Vietnamese mind.

COMRADE DIN We have fought hard to reach this point, comrade. We had to struggle much. Sihanouk drove us into the jungles and the struggle became very difficult, almost insurmountable. We thought we would become extinct. But we survived, because we were rescued.

COMRADE TRAN enters stealthily, and stays away, listening.

COMRADE CHAN Tell me what happened.

COMRADE DIN We tried to survive in the jungles after we left Phnom Penh. We had to eat lizards and leaves, many comrades starved to death. We thought we would have no hope... but we crawled deeper into the caves and found a new comrade.

A SNAKE crawls in and curls up next to COMRADE DIN.

COMRADE DIN We were starving, dying... but deep in the cave, we were fortunate to meet the snake spirit. We begged the snake to help us... we told the snake our mission, that we trying to save our country from the enemy, the foreigners, and needed it's help to save the nation because it was being ruined. And the snake agreed.

    Pause.

The snake saw our wisdom, and thus we made a pact with the snake spirit.

    SNAKE moves head into the lap of COMRADE DIN. He strokes SNAKE affectionately, then cuts it slightly behind its head with a knife and sucks out the blood.

COMRADE DIN The snake fed us when we were hungry, gave us new life to continue the struggle, and now, in return, we give it food. *(glares at SONEE)* Many years ago, the snake made bad karma. Now, by helping us, they have redeemed themselves. We work together to save Kampuchea. The snake taught us how to kill without feeling.

    SNAKE moves off COMRADE DIN's lap. Ever so slowly, COMRADE DIN opens the lid of his box. He reaches in slowly and pulls out a two-headed snake, one head on each end, without a tail. COMRADE CHAN and SONEE stunned.

COMRADE DIN Our partner, the two-headed snake, the king of snakes. Years ago, he killed Muchalinda in a battle in the Cardamom Mountains. Did you hear it? Muchalinda died a terrible death, his bones crushed to dust. The noise enveloped the entire nation. Now he and we control the country. Death serving only itself. Life passes into the mouth - but does not pass out. A hole with a beginning, but no ending. A hole sucking flesh, blood, plants, animals and soil... the entire nation into it's belly. To destroy destruction - eat the night. Wipe out the colony to kill the ant.

> *COMRADE DIN puts snake back in box and closes the lid.*

I think it is time for the snake to eat.

> *Sound of far off lightening, which continues intermittently throughout end of the scene. COMRADE TRAN moves in.*

COMRADE TRAN What's happening here?

COMRADE DIN *(surprised)* Comrade, what are you doing here?

COMRADE TRAN I am on patrol.

COMRADE DIN There is no patrol in this zone.

COMRADE TRAN I am on patrol! What are you doing with him?

COMRADE DIN I am the commander! I ask the questions!

COMRADE TRAN What is the snake doing here?

COMRADE DIN The snake is hungry. The beasts have returned to the forest.

COMRADE TRAN This is not the time or place!

COMRADE DIN I am conducting an interrogation. He made counter-revolutionary statements at the community meeting.

COMRADE TRAN Yes, he said he was hungry.

COMRADE DIN His place is to be hungry.

COMRADE TRAN Not in a true peasant state! The peasants are never hungry!

COMRADE DIN How dare you question Angka!

COMRADE TRAN Angka has betrayed the revolution!
You have betrayed the revolution! You are the counter-
revolutionary!

> *COMRADE CHAN moves to grab COMRADE TRAN, but
> she points her AK-47 at him and he stops.*

COMRADE DIN The king of death is coming, comrade. He
is bringing his little black book. Be careful comrade, be very
careful.

> *Sound of far away battle begins to be heard, artillery and
> bombing, which continues through next scene.*

COMRADE TRAN You have deceived us! Angka has deceived
us! Die, fucking Angka, die!

> *COMRADE TRAN spits on COMRADE DIN, then exits.*

COMRADE CHAN She is an enemy of the people. What do
we do with him?

COMRADE DIN Leave him.

> *SNAKE exits. Battle sounds get louder.*

COMRADE CHAN What's that?

COMRADE DIN Our enemies are pressing closer to us. They
have been infiltrating our border positions and are now in
striking distance.

COMRADE CHAN We must attack! We must attack them
now!

COMRADE DIN The front is calling, comrade. I have seen the white crocodile on the Mehkong. Surely, we will be eaten by tigers or swallowed by crocodiles. Let's go!

COMRADES DIN and CHAN exit. SONEE exits.

Scene Seven

Battle sounds continue. KAN, SOTIE, SOMALIA and WAR SLAVE, carrying bundles and wearing peasant hats, run out, looking for ways to escape. COMRADE CHAN enters.

COMRADE CHAN Where are you going?

WAR SLAVE We were told to run west toward the Cardamom Mountains.

COMRADE CHAN Who gave you these orders?

WAR SLAVE Comrade Tran.

COMRADE CHAN I am in command here. Go east on Route 5.

WAR SLAVE But that is where the bombs are coming from.

COMRADE CHAN Don't worry. Angka will protect you.

WAR SLAVE Comrade, please, there is too much fighting down there.

COMRADE CHAN Angka will protect you. Now go back or I will not be responsible for your safety!

COMRADE TRAN enters.

COMRADE TRAN What's happening here?

COMRADE CHAN These people are trying to go west, but Angka commands that all workers go east to Phnom Penh.

COMRADE TRAN The enemy has attacked from the east. Better to move them west towards the safety of the western zone.

COMRADE CHAN No! I speak for Angka on high!

COMRADE TRAN I have the command here!

COMRADE CHAN *(pointing his gun)* I'll kill them all now!

COMRADE TRAN Yes, comrade, you are right. You have the command here.

> *COMRADE TRAN relaxes then tricks COMRADE CHAN by distracting him and stabs him with a knife. COMRADE CHAN falls to the ground. COMRADE TRAN straddles him and plunges knife repeatedly into his chest. Then she gets up.*

COMRADE TRAN All you people! Go west now! The enemy has attacked from the east.

> *Sound of artillery shells landing closely.*

WAR SLAVE Where should we go?

COMRADE TRAN The dam is breaking to the west, and the waters are flooding out. There is rice there. Perhaps you can go to another country.

> *ALL start to exit.*

KAN Will I ever see you again?

COMRADE TRAN I doubt it.

KAN Why have you been so kind... if you are Khmer Rouge?

COMRADE TRAN *(hesitates)* I'm sorry for everything.

COMRADE TRAN exits.

Scene Eight

WAR SLAVES run from one side of the stage to the other, around the audience if possible, looking for a way out, as battlesounds continue and get louder. Battlesounds segue into chaotic ambient/atmospheric music. WAR SLAVES crash to ground together center stage.

WAR SLAVES slowly and gently pull out black and white photos of relatives and hold them aloft in the air while lying on the ground. They rise slowly while holding pictures, then slowly walk off stage in slow motion in dance-like fashion, with heads bowed.

Lights dim to black. Ambient/atmospheric music sounds fade and jet airplane sound fades in. Then slowly jet sound becomes an idle, and then airport sounds and female voice is heard.

"Welcome to Los Angeles International Airport. All passengers on Korean Air Flight 117 with resident alien status in the United States please proceed to the holding area to the right. I repeat, welcome to Los Angeles International Airport. All passengers on Korean Air Flight 117 with resident alien status..."

Scene Nine

Sound of soft street traffic slowly fades in; lights up to a dim setting. Television comes on playing a blank channel as SONEE, sitting cross-legged on floor in western clothes, watches TV with blank expression. An ashtray with

*numerous burnt out cigarettes and empty pack on the
floor sit in front of him. Various objects on floor, there is
virtually no furniture to speak of. KAN enters casually,
takes off jacket and lets it fall to the floor, walks to TV and
looks at SONEE. Lights slowly fade up to moderate inner
city apartment lighting. KAN turns to address audience
directly.*

KAN He watches TV all day, just sitting there. But he doesn't
really follow it. He just watches the patterns of the lights. Back
home he would quietly watch the cloud patterns changing, the
light shifting, in the late afternoon, after work, and have an
after-work smoke. Here he doesn't work, but he watches the
clouds changing patterns by watching the blank channel on TV.
I really believe he sees the clouds of our country by watching
the blank channel on TV.

We escaped to Thailand after Vietnam invaded. We spent many
years in camps on the border - sites like Khao I Dang, Nong
Chan, Site 2 and Site B - crammed with hundreds of thousands
of people. We were told we could go to a third country. These
places became our sanctuary - then our prison.

Pause.

We were not allowed to farm. We could not leave the camp, we
were surrounded by barbed wire. The Thai would come into the
camp, rob, beat and rape us.

Then we were happy when the United Nations came into the
camp to help us. Their blue flag became our flag of hope. They
said we would go to a different country, and visions of words
like "France" and "America" danced in front of our eyes.

But America is not like we thought, or, maybe I should say our
America is not like we thought their America was thought.
We thought everyone here was rich and nice to us like the
Americans in the camps. But it is too strange for us, and there
is much crime. We are afraid of what we do not understand.

We hear war in sirens and loud noises. When the city was hit by the earthquake we thought Pol Pot was shelling the city. Men who were once brave in battle are now frightened to leave their apartments.

> *COMRADE TRAN enters. Like others, she is dressed in western dress, and drops coat on floor in corner. Likewise, she addresses the audience.*

COMRADE TRAN When the Khmer Rouge first came to our village, we were happy because we thought they would stop the American planes from bombing us, and Lon Nol was no good. They said they were for the peasants; we joined them. Then they turned against us. They took away our freedom and rice, gave us politics and hate. They taught us to hate the city people, and to kill them. Then they turned and hated us. Their politics was a lie. They knew nothing of politics. They knew much about murder. Their politics was the reason they gave for something else. Politics is always the reason for something else.

> *SOMALIA rushes in, wearing jacket, then exits and returns immediately with kitchen knife running out.*

KAN *(blocking SOMALIA)* What are you doing?

SOMALIA He will not get away.

KAN Who will not get away?

SOMALIA Din! Comrade Din! I've seen Comrade Din on the street!

SONEE Din? Comrade Din? *(runs out)*

COMRADE TRAN What? That's not possible!

SOMALIA I've seen Comrade Din on the street, and I'm gonna stab him!

KAN *(blocking SOMALIA)* No you're not. Wait!

COMRADE TRAN Din on the street? That's not possible. I thought he was killed.

SOMALIA I've seen him on the street, and I'm going to do to him what he did to me!

KAN *(grabbing knife at handle)* No, you can't!

SOMALIA Let me go!

KAN Stop it, stop it now!

COMRADE TRAN Put it down!

SOMALIA You're one to talk!

KAN Somalia, give me the knife!

SOMALIA Din must pay, and you'll get it too if you don't get outta my way!

    KAN slaps Somalia lightly then takes knife.

KAN All the killing must stop. We Cambodians must stop fighting amongst ourselves, or we will never have peace.

SOMALIA We can stop later.

KAN What's wrong with now?

SOMALIA Why has this happened to us? Politics is always trouble for the Cambodian people.

COMRADE TRAN It wasn't just politics.

SOMALIA What do you mean it wasn't just politics? They hated us even if we said hello to a foreigner. They were communists sponsored by Vietnam and China!

COMRADE TRAN They were also krou Khmer. They were shamans.

To audience.

Our country is filled with shamans and spirits. The Khmer Rouge were evil shamans, but only a low level power until they made a pact with the evil snake demon that killed the good snake god Muchalinda. They killed Muchalinda and chased away the Naga crocodile. Then the Khmer Rouge and the snake demon destroyed the country together, massacred the population and wiped out   all the other spirits. Only the fish and frog escaped. The Khmer Rouge wanted to destroy everything. To them destruction was... a new god. To clean the country they wanted to destroy it. Keep is no gain. Lose is no loss. They were like a fire burning on a lake, evaporating all the water, until nothing was left. Then the fire would scorch the empty sky... empty of insects, all living things, even ghosts... cold, dark, silent, enormous.

Pause.

I made a mistake joining the Khmer Rouge. Now my karma is bad. I am scared.

KAN I'm sure the gods noticed your kindness, sister.

COMRADE TRAN Sometimes we do things without knowing why. Death is a fish in your hands. Then an eagle swoops down and takes a life dropping my ring into the bottom of the lake. The lake that burns.

Large NAGA CROCODILE SPIRIT crawls in and lays on floor downstage center. All three kneel on the floor around it.

COMRADE TRAN We sink in the waters of millions of souls and hope that the Naga crocodile will keep us from sinking further. We wait for the return of the Naga to Cambodia. We wait to see the white crocodile again on the Mehkong River.

> *Street sounds fade out. Lights become warmer. FISH and*
> *FROG enter (standing on two feet) carrying long incense*
> *sticks and reeds in their hands; the reeds have the black*
> *and white relative photos from the last scene attached to*
> *the top. The incense sticks are already lit. They kneel with*
> *the others around the serpent.*

KAN We wait for the fish to return to the lakes of Cambodia.
We wait for the frog spirits to come back to our village, their
nighttime calls like the ring of marriage, binding man and
nature. We thirst for peace like the baked earth awaits the
monsoon rain. The earth, the rain and the mist of our beautiful
Cambodia beckon us like a thousand year dream.

> *Pause.*

We Khmer are hopeful for our future. But not only for our
future as a nation, but for our future here in America. We now
have a new temple, and go there often to pray. For our departed
ancestors, and for a future.

SOMALIA We can keep our culture alive at the temple. We
will not lose our past that the Khmer Rouge tried to destroy.
Keep is to gain. There is no loss.

COMRADE TRAN We will go to the temple and pray to
heal our country. Our faith in our traditions has helped us to
survive. We will go to the temple now.

> *Moody yet uplifting Cambodian music comes on. The*
> *three women rise and casually collect their jackets, then*
> *exit. After a few seconds, FISH and FROG stand up, with*
> *reeds and incense sticks, behind the NAGA CROCODILE.*
> *The CROCODILE stirs, and begins to rise slightly in a slow*
> *dance. The CROCODILE lumbers off, with the FISH and*
> *FROG following slowly in a moody, linear procession. All*
> *three exit. Lights start to dim as song continues. Stage*

becomes dark. Song continues in the dark, slowly fading, hitting silence on last note of the song.

FINI

TUAL KAN'S JOURNEY

**a symbolic drama about
a Cambodian woman's struggle
to survive in the United States**

Tual Kan's Journey

Tual Kan's Journey premiered on March 17, 1993 at EXIT Theatre in San Francisco, California. The play was directed by the author, who also did the visual design and created the masks and properties. The play was produced by EXIT Theatre, with the following as the original cast and crew:

TUAL KAN	Earlene P. Somera
GRANDMA	Vivian Wu
TERESA	Jennie S. Yee
CAMBODIAN FORTUNE TELLER	Alan Quismorio
FATHER SPIRIT	Steve Uchida
KHMER ROUGE SPIRIT	Alan Quismorio
APSARA SPIRIT	Jennie S. Yee

Sound Design	Tony Avoid
Lighting Design	Rick Garlinghouse
Apsara Spirit Costume	George Adam Renz, San Francisco Costume Bank
Stage Manager	Pippa Rowlandson
Stage Construction	Phyllis de Prieste
Light and Sound Operator	Rick Garlinghouse
Cambodian Performance Interpreter	Sreng Khouch
Photos	Laurie Gallant

Cast of Characters

TUAL KAN, *an adult Cambodian woman*
GRANDMA, *Tual Kan's mother, with grey hair and glasses*
TERESA, *Tual Kan's teenage daughter, dressed in downbeat, dark rap style with Oakland Raiders sports cap*
CAMBODIAN FORTUNE TELLER, *barefoot, dressed casually in rural clothes*
FATHER SPIRIT, *Cambodian farmer*

*KHMER ROUGE SPIRIT, dressed in Khmer Rouge black
with traditional red Cambodian scarf, the kramaa
APSARA SPIRIT, who is dressed and moves like a classical
Cambodian dancer, and is based on the female Apsara
carvings of the Angkor Wat temple complex in Cambodia;
and is invisible to the other characters*

Setting

*A shabby apartment interior in San Francisco's Tenderloin
neighborhood. An alcove leads to apartment's front door,
which is nominally backstage, while a doorway leads to
an offstage kitchen and extra bedroom. Upstage is a single
bed. Walls are a plain, dull yet light color with brighter
pictures and posters of Cambodia, Asian calendars, singers
and stars, and Hindu religious posters. Near the bed is
a traditional spirit house and altar. Photo of father is
prominently displayed on spirit house, along with wilted
flowers and a large pitcher of water. Room is slightly
disheveled, with clothes on floor in corners. Apartment is
spare, dull, yet with bright, well-worn items; it also smells
of ginger, garlic, fried food and incense. A bird cage with a
few birds in it is downstage right.*

Time - 1980s, 1990s

*Lights come up, and APSARA SPIRIT is standing center
stage. In addition to her costume, a decorative gray stone
ring, with gold trim, about 5" in diameter, is on a necklace
over her chest. The ring is patterned after stone ring
necklaces carved into Angkor Wat apsara temple reliefs.
She holds one hand aloft in open-handed traditional
Cambodian dance pose, and the other is clenched into a
fist, held horizontally. She rotates her fist, to a vertical
position, opens it, water drips off, and she flicks her fingers
twice, shooting out water, extending her fingers with each
flick. At the end of second flick, the sound of Cambodian
folk music comes on from kitchen area. Front door is
heard to open and close and TUAL KAN enters. She*

*puts down plastic grocery bags and rests at doorway for
a second. Then she sits on the bed and pulls a small tray
with silver bowls from beside the bed to her, takes betel
nut and powder from the bowls, returns tray, puts the nut
and powder into her mouth, shuts her eyes and chews.
APSARA SPIRIT has been moving gently to sit next to her
on the bed during this sequence, taking the same position
as her.*

*Jungle sounds fade up and blend into the folk music.
FATHER SPIRIT, dressed in traditional Cambodian rural
clothing and carrying a basket, passes by downstage in
slow motion. He wears a Kampuchea Krom hat, his face
is hidden, swathed in scarves, and he pulls wet, bound
rice seedling bundles from the basket and tosses them
downstage. He exits. TUAL KAN opens her eyes. She
walks to the birdcage, reaches into the cage and gently
strokes the birds. APSARA SPIRIT stays sitting on the
bed. Sound of FATHER SPIRIT, speaking in Cambodian, is
heard, along with machine gun fire and distant artillery:*

FATHER SPIRIT Daughter! Daughter! Run away, go now!
Hide in the ditch behind the fields! I will get you later! Go
now! Go!

*TUAL KAN puts her hands to her head, and APSARA
SPIRIT does the same. GRANDMA enters from the
kitchen. Cambodian music and jungle sound piece stops
when she speaks.*

GRANDMA Did you get everything?

TUAL KAN Yes.

*TUAL KAN returns to sit on the bed next to APSARA
SPIRIT.*

GRANDMA *(looking in bags)* No fish?

TUAL KAN They didn't have any today.

GRANDMA What about the banana leaf?

TUAL KAN I got it.

GRANDMA You got the banana leaf but no fish.

TUAL KAN No. Yes.

GRANDMA If we were in Cambodia, we could just go out and get a fish from the lake. Just throw in a net and pull them out.

TUAL KAN We're not in Cambodia. We're in America. We get fish with these.

TUAL KAN puts food stamps under mattress.

GRANDMA I heard there's lots of fish in a place called Stucktun. The lakes are big there, there's many Cambodians and no Pol Pot soldiers.

TUAL KAN Uh-hum.

GRANDMA There's so many fish there people can throw them up in the air. They fly in the clouds just like birds. Some even said they saw the Apsara. The Cambodians in Stucktun are happy.

TUAL KAN So where is Stucktun, mama?

GRANDMA It's near Cambodia.

TUAL KAN How do you know?

GRANDMA Because it's real hot there, just like in Cambodia.

GRANDMA exits to kitchen, carrying bags.

TUAL KAN The snake chased us out of Cambodia - now it's followed us to America.

GRANDMA *(from offstage)* Do you want the som cjake now?

TUAL KAN Yes, mama.

> *GRANDMA enters, she gives som cjake, a banana leaf covered dessert, to TUAL KAN on a Cambodian style silver plate, then exits to the kitchen. TUAL KAN opens the som cjake, and begins to eat it slowly. APSARA SPIRIT gently touches her index finger to the dessert. TUAL KAN looks closer at the dessert, surprised to find and pulls out a ring, about 5" in diameter, identical to the one worn by the APSARA SPIRIT. She lifts it up out of the dessert, but APSARA SPIRIT takes the ring from her and exits, "floating" sideways while facing audience.*

> *GRANDMA enters.*

GRANDMA I can't find a lottery ticket. Did you get one?

TUAL KAN No, I'm sorry.

> *GRANDMA sits on bed.*

TUAL KAN I get nervous in the store. I couldn't remember how to ask for one. I just want to cover myself with this blanket. I just want to pull some big, cold palm leaf branches over me to block out the sun, and hide. The leaves can cool me off like a large "coca-cola." I'm always thirsty.

> *TUAL KAN pours water from pitcher at spirit house into glass and freshens her face. GRANDMA lays down to take a nap. Cambodian music and jungle sounds fade up as before. FATHER SPIRIT enters as before, but this time his face is visible, with white spiral designs on each cheek. In slow motion, he tosses rice seedling bundles as previously.*

TUAL KAN *(standing)* Father! Father! When are you going to be home! Mama wants to know! The palm trees are going to have their babies!

> *Wind sound with chimes comes up in addition to other sounds.*

FATHER SPIRIT Tell mother I'll be back in time for the palm trees. Daughter, I have something important to tell you. I saw a fortune teller yesterday. He said that in the future, our family will have two homes in a foreign country, but none here in Cambodia. Where is your husband?

TUAL KAN He's at the army post today.

FATHER SPIRIT He should pay more attention to what's happening in the countryside.

TUAL KAN Why?

FATHER SPIRIT *(he pulls a seedling bundle, bound with a large ring in the style of the others, from the basket and gives it to her)* Keep this, daughter. I'll be home soon.

> *As FATHER SPIRIT tilts basket, a severed animal head is briefly visible in the bottom of the basket. He gazes carefully to the right and left, then exits and music fades out. TUAL KAN puts the seeding bundle with ring by the spirit house, and carefully pours water from the pitcher over it.*
>
> *Doorway is heard to open and close and rap music is heard and gets louder. TERESA enters, dressed as Western youth in rap style, bright lipstick and carrying boombox.*

TUAL KAN Teresa! Turn it down! Ssshhh! Grandma's trying to sleep.

TERESA Looks like she's sleeping to me.

TUAL KAN She can hear it. It'll wake her up.

TERESA She can't hear it when she's asleep.

TUAL KAN Yes, she can.

TERESA People can't hear things when they're asleep. It's a type of subconsciousness, a state of being, ya know?

TUAL KAN We don't like that kind of music around here.

TERESA Yes we do, we like it very much. Me, myself, and I.

TUAL KAN You shouldn't like it. It's not your kind of music. You should like Cambodian music.

TERESA *(checking fingernails)* Yo, moms, that old farmer music really sucks.

> GRANDMA *groans and babbles in her sleep briefly, turns over, swiping at imaginary flies.*

TUAL KAN That "old farmer music" is the music of your ancestors.

TERESA I don't have any ancestors.

TUAL KAN I'm sure you could remember them if you tried.

TERESA I don't. Can't.

TUAL KAN Well, you should.

TERESA Why? I was just a baby. You never tell me anything about them anyway.

TUAL KAN But what about the photos of your grandfather?

TERESA Where are the photos of my father?

TUAL KAN *(pause)* Turn that music off! *(grabs boom box and turns it off)*

> TERESA turns to leave.

TUAL KAN Where do you think you're going?

TERESA To the Rec Center!

TUAL KAN No you're not! You're staying here.

TERESA Why?

TUAL KAN You can help us around the house.

TERESA I can't do nuthin'.

TUAL KAN You can fill out our welfare forms.

TERESA Fill it out yourself!

TUAL KAN I can't read English!

TERESA Then learn it, goddammit!

TUAL KAN *(grabs her by the hair, pulling her)* I'm your mother and you will not talk to me like that! You're in this family and this is a Cambodian family, not an American family. And in a Cambodian family, we stay together and work together. Just like in the village.

TERESA I don't remember no "village." I was brought up in a god, damn refugee camp. I don't know no fuckin' village!

> TERESA runs off to offstage bedroom. TUAL KAN follows
> her. GRANDMA wakes up. As the following dialogue
> is heard offstage, KHMER ROUGE SPIRIT enters the

apartment. He is dressed in Khmer Rouge black, with red scarf and AK-47 rifle. He stealthily looks apartment over, especially noticing seedling bundle with ring near the spirit house, and the bird cage. GRANDMA watches him fuzzily.

TUAL KAN *(offstage)* Sweetheart, I'm sorry. Listen to me. Grandma and I need you. You don't know the village, but it's all that Grandma and I do know. Gentle wind blowing like crystals, palm and fruit trees filled with their pregnancy, perfectly clear water, laughter from behind the temples... this is the Cambodia we know, and we are Cambodian. You are Cambodian, too.

TERESA Why do I wanna be Cambodian? All I know about Cambodia is Khmer Rouge, everybody's killing everybody else, a million heads stuck on poles, soldiers with insect faces! All the kids at school are afraid of me! I don't wanna be no "Cambodian."

TERESA and TUAL KAN enter. KHMER ROUGE SPIRIT slips out.

TUAL KAN So what do you want to be?

TERESA I'm down with my homeboys.

Sound fades in at low volume, intermittent sounds of village life: birds chirping, gentle conversation passing as people walk by, gas-powered farm tools heard lowly in the distance.

GRANDMA Teresa, sweetheart... you should be what you already are. You look like an American girl, but underneath you are still Cambodian... you have the sweet juice of Cambodia's forests in you, the Mehkong River flows in these sweet arms, Tonle Sap lake sits at your belly, and the apsara goddess of Angkor Wat, she's in your heart. The Khmer Rouge are not Cambodian. They are from Vietnam and China. They were snakes who devoured the Cambodian people. Cambodia is rice field mirrors, you look in the sky and you see the apsara spirit above you in the clouds, then she comes down and carries you to the next village to meet your future husband, he comes out of the forest and he is shining; he walks towards you and all the village smells cling to him, a perfume; his skin, as smooth as a bird's stare, his smile, you can hear his heart beating, trees pulse, buffalos walk, and the animals can talk, it's a magic; then you and he fly through the clouds to your privacy. This is Cambodia, and this is how I met your grandfather.

TERESA *(softly)* Whatever.

TUAL KAN I feel sorry for you.

GRANDMA Well, she doesn't remember anything about Cambodia, her father or her grandfather. Maybe this is the end or our family, just a bunch of banana skins in a chicken yard.

TUAL KAN She's impossible, mama. I don't know what to do with her. She's like a chicken swimming across a river.

TERESA A chicken swimming across a river.

TUAL KAN A chicken swimming across a river.

TERESA A chicken, swimming across a river!

TUAL KAN A chicken, swimming across a river!

GRANDMA If we were in Cambodia, she'd have no problems.

TERESA If we were in Cambodia, I'd be dead. Just like grandpa. Just another ghost.

GRANDMA What do you know about your grandfather? Nothing!

Cambodian music comes on. During this next speech,

FATHER SPIRIT, sweaty and dirty, enters. His hands are bound behind him with a leather thong, and as he reaches mid-stage, thong is seen to be dragging a severed buffalo's head. He struggles to pull it. Following head, KHMER ROUGE SPIRIT walks slowly. TERESA and GRANDMA watch this scene during GRANDMA'S speech.

GRANDMA One of the first things the Khmer Rouge did was to use your grandfather as a buffalo to pull the plow. They hooked him up to the plow, and the Khmer Rouge rode on the back of it so he had to pull the plow and the soldier. Then the Khmer Rouge would whip him and whip him, and everything I knew became hell that day. They planted something, I don't know what it was. I had to hold in my tears, or they would torture me too. That night his back was cut open like a slashed open palm tree trunk; he burned like the fire ants.

KHMER ROUGE SPIRIT and FATHER SPIRIT exit. Music fades out.

TERESA Grandma, what happened to my dad?

GRANDMA Teresa, I...

TERESA Yeah, right, Teresa I! Teresa I! All the kids at school say I don't even have a father! They call me a bastard! They say mama was a prostitute in the camps! I'm the only kid without a father!

TERESA runs out.

TUAL KAN Mama. We've been abandoned by Cambodia, Buddha, everybody.

GRANDMA That's not true.

TUAL KAN I can't do anything. I can't even buy a lottery ticket. *(TUAL KAN goes to the birdcage)* Why did everybody die but we survived? Why were we allowed to live but then sent over here, stuck in a foreign country, a nightmare?

GRANDMA It must be our karma.

TUAL KAN Our karma?

GRANDMA Our good karma. It saved us. We weren't killed. We're still alive. Remember what we used to say? Better to be a dog in America than a "comrade" in Kampuchea?

TUAL KAN Sometimes I wish - I'd died in Cambodia with the others. If we died there, our family would be together. Now there's an ocean of time between us.

GRANDMA Don't say such foolishness. You must live to carry on the family name, and protect your daughter. You're his and my daughter, and you must carry on our family name. Our country was destroyed. But many of us ran away, and we are like... birds, little birds... and we flew away to another country. We are only birds...

TUAL KAN We are like birds.

GRANDMA We are like little birds. Is there anything better than that?

Pause. TUAL KAN moves to the upstage bed.

TUAL KAN I'm sorry mama. I'm a bad mother. You should have left me in the ditch behind the field. I'd never heard noises as loud as that battle. So loud, you thought hell's wind shot through. When it started, father put Teresa and me in the ditch. He said the Khmer Rouge were attacking the village.

GRANDMA Tual, don't do this to yourself.

TUAL KAN moves downstage. During this next speech, soft, low volume sounds of gentle wind fades in intermittently, with blank spaces in between.

TUAL KAN Then father left. He said he would come back
later, so I stayed there. The noise of the fighting went on,
shooting and explosions and people yelling, our buffalo got
hit by something, cried for so long, then stopped. The moon
cracked. I pulled branches over us to hide.   Then somebody
jumped in the ditch with us. I was so scared, they put their
hand over my mouth, but then I saw it was Rouen. I had
never been so happy to see my husband. It started raining,
and we stayed there so long. Then, all these bugs came out,
and completely covered us. Thousands and thousands of bugs,
crawling all over us, and carrying these dead birds they were
eating. Just bugs and bugs and chewing and eating and chewing
and eating and chewing and eating in my ears, my eyes, my
mouth and under my sarong. Then the battle sound stopped.
And I was so thirsty. I heard voices. The Khmer Rouge were
looking for people. And I heard father's voice. The Khmer
Rouge were asking him where Rouen was. He said he didn't
know. They said "we know he's your son-in-law, where is he?"
and they were cutting him with a knife, and he was screaming.
I wanted to say something, I looked at Rouen, but he wasn't
beside me anymore. He was on the other side of the ditch... his
face... like a newborn babies face - he was going to run away.
You could hear father screaming, but Rouen ran away. He ran
into the forest, and I never say him again.

   Pause.

Then the Khmer Rouge looked into the ditch and saw me with
my baby. I saw father. He was bleeding. They asked him who I
was, he said he didn't know. I wanted to say something, but the
look in his eyes - like an old ax with a wooden handle – said be
quiet. They hit him on the head with a rifle, and said they were
going to shoot him for betraying the fatherland.

   *TUAL KAN goes to the spirit house and slowly refreshes
   herself with water from the pitcher, then sits on the bed.*

TUAL KAN I used to be so proud of Rouen in his uniform.

So strong, so handsome. I knew all the girls in the village were jealous of me. When he held me in his arms in that uniform, I'd never loved anyone so much in my life.

GRANDMA Tual, don't blame him for leaving you. He wanted to live. He wanted to survive, for his family, for his country. They would have executed him, you know that. He is a bird too. A bird among many birds. There are many. Many many.

> *GRANDMA takes father's picture from spirit house and gently puts it in the bird cage. TUAL KAN leans against wall. TERESA enters.*

TERESA What's wrong?

GRANDMA Something's bad with your mother. She's sick.

TUAL KAN I need to get out of here.

TERESA Where you gonna go? Gonna get another lottery ticket?

> *GRANDMA glares at TERESA.*

TERESA Sorry.

TUAL KAN I need to get out of this apartment. My life.

TERESA Where would we go? Mission? Bayview?

TUAL KAN We'll never get back to Cambodia.

GRANDMA Sweetheart, maybe we could go to ...Stucktun.

TERESA Where?

GRANDMA Stucktun.

TERESA Stucktun?

GRANDMA Yes, yes.

TERESA What's a Stucktun?

GRANDMA A city with many Cambodians.

TERESA Jesus, Grandma, it's called Stockton.

GRANDMA "Stawktawn." Tual, we can go to "Stawktawn."

TUAL KAN I don't know.

GRANDMA Life is better there.

TERESA It's boring there.

GRANDMA Life is better there.

TERESA It's boring. It's really, really boring! LA is better!

GRANDMA LA is dangerous!

TERESA What?

GRANDMA The Khmer Rouge are in LA!

TERESA How do you know?

GRANDMA Somebody saw it on TV.

TERESA I can't believe this shit.

GRANDMA The houses are all spread out in Stucktun, there's more trees, lakes, fish, the aspara.

TUAL KAN Mama, you're being silly, there is no aspara.

GRANDMA We can get the fish, have a garden, and there's no Khmer Rouge there. They have rice field mirrors and the buffalos can talk to you.

TUAL KAN Mama, how're we gonna get there? Take the bus? And how will we pay for it?

GRANDMA I'll make a dinner for the bus driver!

TERESA My God!

GRANDMA Yes, Cambodians are happier in Stucktun.

TUAL KAN Well, maybe if we...

GRANDMA If we were in Stucktun, you'd be fine. We should get that fortune teller. He knows everything. He can tell what's wrong with you.

TUAL KAN Nothing's wrong with me. We don't need that fortune teller.

GRANDMA I'm going to get him anyway. He can tell us if our destiny is to go to Stucktun! Go get me a bag from the kitchen.

> *TERESA goes into the kitchen and comes back with a brown paper shopping bag. GRANDMA goes to the birdcage and takes a bird out, then puts it in the bag.*

GRANDMA Go put it outside in the hallway.

> *TERESA groans and exits. We hear the front door open and then close a second later. Then TERESA returns and goes off to the offstage bedroom.*

TUAL KAN Mama, maybe it's not a good idea to go to Stockton. We don't know anybody there.

GRANDMA Don't worry Tual.

TUAL KAN But mama...

GRANDMA Tual, don't worry.

Pause.

TUAL KAN So should we call that fortune teller and tell him we want to speak to him?

A loud knock is heard at the front door.

GRANDMA *(smiling)* Go to the door, Tual, go to the door.

> *TUAL KAN exits and the front door is heard to open, and then close a moment later. She returns to the room holding the shopping bag. She pulls a large fish out of the bag. The front door is heard to open. The FORTUNE TELLER enters. He wears plain, rumpled well-worn clothes and is barefoot, has three large brick-red blotches on his forehead from coining. Smoke seems to be hovering over and following him. During the next scene, the sound of soft, low volume wind blows intermittently.*

GRANDMA *(grinning)* Thank you for coming.

FORTUNE TELLER I got a message that... *(grins briefly)* I heard you needed to see me.

GRANDMA Yes, thank you for coming to see us. Please sit down.

> *All three sit on the floor center stage, TUAL KAN putting the shopping bag to the side with the fish. After a pause, GRANDMA looks to the two others in succession, then grins broadly and sheepishly, nodding her head. After another pause, TUAL KAN looks to the two others, then grins broadly and sheepishly, nodding her head. After another pause, all three grin broadly and sheepishly, nodding to each other at the same time.*

GRANDMA Have you been busy?

FORTUNE TELLER Oh, a healing here, a reading there - I had to do an exorcism at McDonald's - very difficult - fries and burger smell - terrible. We made a mess - you know how it is. What can I do for you?

GRANDMA This is my daughter. She's sick. I've heard that life is better in Stucktun. I think she'll be better there. We want to go to Stucktun.

FORTUNE TELLER Ah yes, many Cambodian people there - many fish! *(chuckles)*

GRANDMA Is Stucktun nearer to Cambodia?

FORTUNE TELLER *(pauses, then shakes head meaningfully)* Well, since Cambodia's directly on the other side of the world according to latitude and longitude, in any direction you go, you would be nearer to Cambodia, as the crow flies; so, yes, Stockton is nearer to Cambodia.

GRANDMA I knew it. We want to move there. We hear life's better there, there's more open space than here. Please, tell us if it's in our fortune to move to Stucktun.

FORTUNE TELLER I see. I'll see what I can find out.

> *FORTUNE TELLER rolls up shirt sleeves to reveal arms heavily tattooed in Cambodian style. He produces a small chalkboard and quickly writes numerous figures on it. As he does this, APSARA SPIRIT enters and assumes "listening" posture. FORTUNE TELLER rises from floor, produces a cigarette lighter from his pocket, lights it, and, holding the lighter aloft, circumnavigates the room. He stops near APSARA SPIRIT. APSARA SPIRIT changes from listening posture to a "praying" posture. FORTUNE TELLER flicks lighter off, then sits back down.*

FORTUNE TELLER How old are you?

GRANDMA 60.

> *FORTUNE TELLER turns board over, and we see it is full of figures. He quickly counts to the 60th figure.*

FORTUNE TELLER You'll get to where you want to go, but not necessarily with who you think. A house that was destroyed in Cambodia actually was not destroyed. A house that can float on a river can also sail across an ocean. Call the birds, so that all the birds will return to the bird house. Have you noticed anything unusual lately?

GRANDMA No. Does that mean we'll get to Stucktun?

FORTUNE TELLER I can't tell you whether you'll get to Stockton or not. But I can tell you this. Somebody's trying to get in touch with you.

TUAL KAN Who?

FORTUNE TELLER Your father.

TUAL KAN My father?

FORTUNE TELLER Your father. He's not dead.

GRANDMA Oh!

FORTUNE TELLER He's not dead. He's still alive. He needs you.

TUAL KAN Me?

FORTUNE TELLER You.

TUAL KAN What am I supposed to do?

FORTUNE TELLER That's all I can say. A pineapple lives longer staying on the tree.

> *FORTUNE TELLER moves toward TUAL KAN and stares deeply at her, trying to look inside her. GRANDMA reaches under bed's mattress and gets a few dollars and puts them in FORTUNE TELLER'S hand; ushering him toward the door.*

GRANDMA Thank you for your help.

FORTUNE TELLER My pleasure. Good luck to you all. *(grins)* "Dam doeum go." Oh, by the way, they've got fish at the market now. "Dam doeum go." *(repeats phrase and chuckles on his way out)*

> *FORTUNE TELLER exits and GRANDMA follows him to the door. We hear the door open and close, then GRANDMA reappears and rushes to spirit altar and prays fervently.*

GRANDMA My husband's alive! *(cries)* The apsara must've helped him in the forest! The Khmer Rouge couldn't shoot him!

> *Sound of a loud bump at the front door.*

GRANDMA Maybe that's him!

> *GRANDMA rushes off. Muffled sounds and a large thud heard from front door area. Then strange scratching noises and sounds are heard. GRANDMA enters dazed without glasses and blood trickling from her mouth. She collapses on floor center stage. Murky, nightmarish spook sound piece starts.*

TUAL KAN Mama! Mama!

> *Sound piece continues as TUAL KAN struggles to drag*

GRANDMA *away.*

TUAL KAN Teresa! Help! Help! Teresa!

*Sound of scuffling and strange nightmarish sound piece
continues. Sounds of shooting and distant artillery fades
up into the mix.*

TUAL KAN Whoever you are, please go away! We are birds,
just poor little birds, only birds!

*Lights dim to nightmarish blue-green tinged garish look. A
flickering violent light and thumping battle sounds come
from foyer. Ground-hugging smoke is seen coming out of
foyer into entrance.*

TUAL KAN *(covering GRANDMA'S body with her own)* Go
ahead and kill me if you want! Crush me like a bug, crack me
like a stick, burn me like an old, broken cart, just let my bones
sing in silence! Is that all I have to ask?

*TUAL KAN collapses over GRANDMA. Murky,
disturbing soundpiece continues, but battle sounds fade out
soon.*

*With ground-hugging fog flushing in, KHMER ROUGE
SPIRIT enters. His face and shoulders are splattered with
blood, and he wears a snakehead medallion as a necklace
over his chest, and he moves as an apparition, not a
person, and poses idol-like. A thong in his hand leads
offstage. This entire movement section is performed in a
dream-like, start-stop fashion, and smoke swirls around.*

*APSARA SPIRIT takes the large ring off of the seedling
bundle near the spirit house; she taps TUAL KAN on top
of her head, and TUAL KAN revives. She gives the ring to
TUAL KAN, who holds the ring aloft as a kind of talisman.*

As APSARA SPIRIT moves to take "listening" posture,

KHMER ROUGE SPIRIT tugs on thong and FATHER SPIRIT, bloodied a bit and tied to the thong, spins quickly to center stage, then stops, idol-like. TUAL KAN moves slowly to FATHER SPIRIT and ritualistically dabs clean his bloody wound with her shirt sleeve.

TUAL KAN gets rice seedling bundle from spirit house and puts it in FATHER SPIRIT'S hands.

TUAL KAN disattaches the thong, puts it around her own neck, and turns, facing away from KHMER ROUGE SPIRIT, and leans in this direction. KHMER ROUGE SPIRIT pulls on thong and TUAL KAN slowly moves backwards towards him. APSARA SPIRIT leads FATHER SPIRIT away to right; FATHER SPIRIT opens mouth and a white flower pops out. APSARA SPIRIT takes flower and holds it high in the air; APSARA SPIRIT brushes GRANDMA with the flower, GRANDMA revives, and APSARA SPIRIT exits, followed by FATHER SPIRIT and GRANDMA.

The sound piece peaks. KHMER ROUGE SPIRIT pulls TUAL KAN closer, spins her around, grabs her and cuts her on the neck so she bleeds. TUAL KAN holds her ring aloft, and, reaching through the ring's center hole, grasps the KHMER ROUGE SPIRIT'S snakehead medallion and pulls it off him, back through the hole in the ring; and holds it aloft.

TUAL KAN moves off and exits. KHMER ROUGE SPIRIT drifts backwards, as if pulled by an unseen force, back through the alcove and disappears.

Sound changes into soft, exquisitely lyrical traditional Cambodian music at loud volume, emphasized with a lovely, repetitive beat on traditional mallet-struck orchestral instruments.

A giant, human-sized bird walks out gingerly from

doorway, barely fitting through the door. It stands in place rocking slightly to the music.

APSARA SPIRIT follows with a large, 2' diameter ring balanced on her head, and a glass with a small ring in it. She carefully puts the glass in the birdcage.

TUAL KAN and GRANDMA, wearing traditional Cambodian farmer clothing, including kramaa scarves, enter. They are younger, as they would have appeared 15 years ago, GRANDMA is without glasses and hair is much darker. They carry silver vases filled with water, and their hair and faces are streaked with water. Smiling and facing downstage, they flick water from their fingers onto the audience.

FATHER SPIRIT enters and moves to center stage. APSARA SPIRIT exits behind him into doorway, followed by the giant bird. TUAL KAN and GRANDMA move to encircle FATHER SPIRIT who is standing center stage and waving slowly. TUAL KAN and GRANDMA begin to laugh, then throw water from vases onto FATHER SPIRIT. Lights immediately dim out, and music slowly fades out in the darkness.

Lights up. TUAL KAN enters, carrying the ring in her hands and examining it. TERESA and GRANDMA enter simultaneously.

TERESA Where'd you get that?

TUAL KAN I've had it for a long time.

GRANDMA I've never seen it before.

TUAL KAN I guess I'd lost it.

TERESA What is it?

TUAL KAN Something from Cambodia that I used to have a long time ago.

TERESA Hm.

TUAL KAN Mama?

GRANDMA Yes?

TUAL KAN We should go to Stockton.

GRANDMA Yes...sweetheart, yes. Yes!

TERESA Go to Stockton?

TUAL KAN Yes. Get out of this apartment. Get out of this neighborhood.

TERESA This neighborhood's down!

TUAL KAN You're right it's down. Very down. We've got to move to Stockton. I can't explain it. But I feel our family's destiny is in Stockton.

TERESA What's that supposed to mean?

TUAL KAN I think your grandfather's in Stockton.

GRANDMA I had a dream last night. Your father was with us. He was all wet from crying with happiness. We were wet too!

TUAL KAN Mama, go pack a few bags. We'll leave right now.

GRANDMA Well...

TUAL KAN Yes, right now. Now.

GRANDMA pauses.

TUAL KAN Go!

GRANDMA Oh!

> *GRANDMA exits.*

TERESA Leave now? Right now?

TUAL KAN You've got to do something when the time is right.

TERESA I don't wanna go to no Stockton!

TUAL KAN Why not?

TERESA I won't have any friends there, I won't have nuthin' to do.

TUAL KAN It'll be better than here. Our life will be better. I'll make it better. Your family, your line, is moving there. You have to go. Whether we see your father again or not, we can't sit here and wait for things to happen to us, we've got to go out and make things happen for us. And we're getting out of this apartment.

GRANDMA *(offstage)* Teresa, can you help me in here?

> *TERESA goes off. Following dialogue is heard offstage while TUAL KAN continues to examine her ring.*

TERESA Do we need all this stuff in Stockton?

GRANDMA Of course. We need to cook and eat.

TERESA They better have McDonald's out there.

GRANDMA Of course they do. This is America, isn't it? But I can cook better than McDonald's.

TERESA Actually those fries you made last week were

righteous.

GRANDMA See. I told you. I'll feed you so you can get big and fat. I'll feed you like an old water buffalo.

TERESA You'll feed me hay?

GRANDMA Why not?

> *GRANDMA and TERESA enter. TERESA is weighted down with huge bags over her shoulders, GRANDMA has bags and a big bag of aluminum cans.*

GRANDMA Will we be late for the bus?

TUAL KAN Don't worry mama. The bus leaves every hour from Mission. We'll be in Stockton today.

GRANDMA There's not many fish in America, but they sure have a lot of cans.

TUAL KAN You look real good like that.

TERESA I do not.

TUAL KAN Here, let's put another one on top.

> *TUAL KAN puts bag of cans on top of TERESA's other bags.*

TERESA Mama, jesus! Grandma, tell her to stop!

TUAL KAN She's looking more and more like a water buffalo everyday.

GRANDMA I'm going to feed her hay.

TUAL KAN Good. Then she'll smell like one too.

TERESA Bull!... I mean...

TUAL KAN Even got that big cow butt.

> *TUAL KAN kicks TERESA playfully.*

TERESA Stop it, god... !

> *TUAL KAN helps her take off bundles and bags.*

TERESA What's this?

> *TERESA takes ring out of the glass in the birdcage.*

TUAL KAN We need to take that.

TERESA What is it?

TUAL KAN It's... mama when she makes som cjake. Me when I planted rice. Cambodian people... when we make music, sew clothes, harvest rice, tend animals, go to temple. It'll help us survive in Stockton.

GRANDMA The soft breeze of red laquered sunsets.

TUAL KAN We're descendants of the people of Angkor Wat. The strength in their stones feeds the rivers in our bodies. We've lived through hell - have felt the whip and teeth of the demon, the cave of a day without sunlight, the silent space left by a life taken without meaning. This is easy! Moving to Stockton. Nothing was as bad as the Khmer Rouge. Nothing. Keep it with you. It'll give you strength - if you let it.

> *TUAL KAN puts necklace around TERESA'S neck.*
> *GRANDMA takes picture of father out of the bird cage.*

GRANDMA Maybe I will see him again.

TERESA I'm scared.

GRANDMA Of what?

TERESA I don't know! Stockton, a new place... everything.

GRANDMA The last time we had to travel like this was when we escaped to Thailand. We had to carry you, you were just a baby. This time you can walk if you have to.

TERESA You mean we're not gonna take the bus??!? Stockton's 200 miles away!

TUAL KAN We're taking the bus. Let's go.

GRANDMA One minute.

> *GRANDMA lights incense and places incense stick in front of spirit altar. She goes onto knees to pray. TUAL KAN joins her then TERESA does also, tentatively. Then GRANDMA and others rise and pick up bags.*

TERESA Will we ever... get back to Cambodia?

TUAL KAN Let's get to Stockton first. Besides... it's closer.

> *All three exit.*

> *Pause.*

> *APSARA SPIRIT enters. She carries large 2' ring over her head. She moves slowly to center stage, lowers ring onto the ground in front of her, and sompeahs (bows) in traditional Cambodian style at one quarter speed. Lights dim as she bows.*

> *FINI*

RETURN TO ANGKOR

**a symbolic drama about
a woman returning to the temples
of her homeland**

Return to Angkor

Return to Angkor premiered on November 3, 1994 at EXIT Theatre in San Francisco, California. The piece was directed and the masks and props were created by the author except for the stage right Goddess figure, which was created by Mrs. Sith Ouch. The play was produced by EXIT Theatre, and supported by a New Theatre Works Regranting Project grant received from Intersection for the Arts. The following is the original cast and crew:

SOPHIE	Earlene Somera
GHOST	Monique Le
MOTHER	Karen Lee
DAUGHTER	Mai Huynh
GUARD	Jim Chin
BLINDFOLDED GHOST, BLACK DOG SOLDIER	
	Marcial Sales

Sound Design	Gil Doyle, High Note Productions
Lighting Design, Sound and Light operator	Rick Garlinghouse
Technician	Christopher Reiter
Props Manager	Marcial Sales
Cambodian Community Outreach	Thou Ny
Temple Head Construction	Richard Ciccarelli & Mark Knego
Goddess Figure originally created by	Mrs. Sith Ouch
Flowers courtesy of	ROSExpress
Photos	Laurie Gallant
Box Office	Olivia Competente

Cast of Characters

SOPHIE, a young, Americanized Cambodian woman who has lived many years in the United States. She is dressed in dark hip hop fashion, with an Oakland Raiders cap.

DAUGHTER, *Cambodian village girl*
MOTHER, *the girl's mother*
GHOST, *ghost of Sophie's sister, who moves in ghostly dance-like way*
GUARD, *male civilian guard who works at the temple complex*
BLINDFOLDED GHOST, *male companion to the female ghost*
BLACK DOG SOLDIER, *wearing a black dog helmet mask, black clothing, red Cambodian kramaa scarf, tire sandals and machine gun*

Stage Set

A temple in Cambodia's Angkor Wat temple complex. Upstage, a large stone Buddha head towers over a clearing center stage; there is an archway under the head leading backstage. The clearing, being in a jungle area, is covered with leaves; and there is a small stone pool, about 2' in diameter, filled with water downstage. A statue of a female Goddess figure, about 5' tall, in the style of Uma, is stage right; with a small, corroded mirror resting at it's base, and a few stone fragments on the ground. There are exits downstage left and upstage left in addition to the exit under the temple head arch. Lighting and sound are expressionistic as the scene demands. Jungle sounds are the background, with soft birds chirping and cooing intermittently. Cambodian folk and pop music should be used as much as possible in the background and foreground, to present a seamless soundscape.

Time - The present.

Lights up to reveal temple setting.

DAUGHTER, dressed in well-worn peasant clothes, in a long, faded, floral Cambodian style skirt, is downstage on her knees by the pool. Standing directly behind her is the GHOST, who carries an old, 8x10 framed picture, a

*portrait of a young girl, cradled in her arms. The GHOST
is dressed in pale, faded clothes, also a traditional skirt; her
face and long, loose hair caked with dust and leaves.*

*DAUGHTER gently and briefly puts water from the pool
on her face, touching her face with the water, but not quite
washing herself.*

DAUGHTER Somebody come from far away with old picture.
Thousands of old pictures, burning and hot, buried all over the
place. All over my country.

*Mid tempo Cambodian folk dance music, the romvong,
starts. DAUGHTER dances a gentle folk dance to the
music, and sways from side to side with her hands in the
air as she dances a circle around the pool. After one circle,
she drifts off through the upstage arch, GHOST exits in
slow, melliflous dance move.*

*SOPHIE enters. She's dressed in contemporary 90's
American hip hop youth style, with long black hair,
Oakland Raiders cap, a loose shirt, lipstick and make-up,
with an analog camera around her neck. She photographs
the upstage temple face, then notices the goddess figure
and the small mirror at its base. Jungle sounds fade up
into the dance music as DAUGHTER enters. The dance
music cross-fades into slow, female-vocal romantic pop,
which becomes part of the background soundscape with
the jungle sounds.*

DAUGHTER Do you have any water? I need water.

SOPHIE No.

DAUGHTER Where you from?

SOPHIE America.

DAUGHTER America? Ooh! America! How big's your

airplane?

SOPHIE My what?

DAUGHTER Your airplane. Did you come in the big plane?

SOPHIE Yeah.

DAUGHTER So how big is it?

SOPHIE It's... real big.

DAUGHTER Ooh! Why'd you come here?

SOPHIE To see the temples.

DAUGHTER No. Why'd you come to our country.

SOPHIE To look for my sister.

DAUGHTER You from around here?

SOPHIE Yeah.

DAUGHTER You don't look like it to me.

SOPHIE I've been in the States for 15 years.

DAUGHTER Do all the American girls look like you?

SOPHIE No.

DAUGHTER *(reaching towards SOPHIE)* Can I try your lipstick?

SOPHIE Listen, are you from around here?

DAUGHTER Yeah.

SOPHIE I'm looking for my sister. This is a picture of her.
Have you ever seen this girl?

SOPHIE shows small photograph to DAUGHTER.

DAUGHTER Hmmm. Looks kinda like me. Pretty.

SOPHIE Have you ever seen anybody who looks like her?

DAUGHTER No.

SOPHIE If you see anybody who looks like her, tell that her
sister is looking for her.

DAUGHTER Everybody's looking for somebody they know.
Half the country's looking for the other half of the country.
Problem is, half the country's dead. Half the country's a ghost.

> *SOPHIE sits on stone fragment and photographs the
> goddess statue. Leaves upstage left begin to stir. A hand
> comes out of the leaves and stone, and GHOST appears
> and starts to move towards SOPHIE. GHOST is carrying
> the framed picture as before, and now we see that it is a
> photo of SOPHIE at an early age. DAUGHTER becomes
> very alert, and seems to sense the presence of GHOST.*

SOPHIE I'd swear I've seen this mirror before.

> *SOPHIE takes a second photo of the goddess statue.
> GHOST sits next to SOPHIE, on SOPHIE'S upstage left
> side, and leans the picture against her thigh. GHOST
> caresses SOPHIE'S hair gently, then takes out a bright,
> plastic child's comb and begins combing SOPHIE'S hair.*

DAUGHTER Were you close to your sister?

SOPHIE We were real close. We grew up together. We would
sit in the yard behind our house in the village and she would
comb my hair. We were playing "madame." I was the rich lady,

and she was the maid. Then we'd switch, and I'd comb her hair and help her get ready for the big dance. We always played with each other cause our ages were real close. We hugged each other when we were hiding from the fighting. I love her, ya know what I'm sayin'?

DAUGHTER How long have you kept that picture?

SOPHIE 15 years.

DAUGHTER Old picture's dangerous.

SOPHIE Why?

DAUGHTER Old picture's the past. Sometimes better to forget than remember.

> *SOPHIE rises and continues looking around the whole area. GHOST slowly exits.*

MOTHER *(heard offstage)* Sweetheart, where are you? Sweetheart?

DAUGHTER Over here, mama.

MOTHER Sweetheart.

DAUGHTER I only wanted some water, mama. I was looking for some water.

MOTHER Mommie's got some nice water for you.

DAUGHTER Mommie's got nice water?

> *MOTHER enters. She's dressed in similar rural Cambodian fashion, carrys a plastic water jug, a canvas bag and smokes a large, hand-rolled cigar.*

MOTHER Mommie's got nice water for... where you from?

DAUGHTER takes water jug and drinks from it quickly.

SOPHIE I'm from the States.

MOTHER Ooh! The States. The United States of America! How big's your airplane?

SOPHIE *(shocked)* Big. Real, real big. Huge. Yeah. Right on.

MOTHER Are you the pilot?

SOPHIE Uh... yeah... yeah! I'm the pilot.

MOTHER Ooh, you are very, very smart... and a beautiful girl, too. You must have a lot of money. You're lucky to be an American. You can buy anything you want. Tell me about America.

SOPHIE It's OK. It's cool. It's down. Everything's real big. Big buildings, big cars. They got everything there... lotsa TVs, VCRs, cassette players...and hair dryers.

MOTHER We got hair dryers. What else?

SOPHIE Washing machines.

MOTHER We got those in town. What else?

SOPHIE We got irons.

MOTHER We got irons too. What else you got?

SOPHIE Uh... motorcycles.

MOTHER Motorcycles we got! What else.

SOPHIE Gas stations.

MOTHER What else. What else. What else!

SOPHIE Uh... Swiss army knives!

MOTHER Ridiculous.

SOPHIE French cheese!

MOTHER *(makes face and spits)* Come on, what else?

SOPHIE Electric... can openers!

MOTHER Electric can openers?

SOPHIE It's a machine that opens cans real fast, so you don't have to open them by hand.

MOTHER Oooh. Aaaah! Heh-heh. Very clever, you Americans. We could use those on the farm to open cans of pesticide.

DAUGHTER To open cans of pesticide!

MOTHER Tell me... is America close to France?

SOPHIE No.

MOTHER So where is America then?

SOPHIE It's... between Mexico and Canada. Yeah. Mexico and Canada.

MOTHER Mexico and Canada? Mexico and Canada! Never heard of them.

SOPHIE They're big countries.

MOTHER Very big, I'm sure.

SOPHIE Yeah.

MOTHER So Mexico and Canada are near each other.

SOPHIE Sort of.

MOTHER So where do you live in the States? New York? Los Angeles!

SOPHIE In San Francisco, a pretty big city. I'm a homegirl, and I'm down. Have you heard of it?

MOTHER Is it near Stockton?

SOPHIE Stockton?

MOTHER Yes. Stockton!

SOPHIE Yeah, it's kinda near Stockton.

MOTHER Very nice.

SOPHIE I'm sure. Look, I'm from around here. I came back to look for my sister. I haven't seen her in 15 years. Have you ever seen this girl?

> *SOPHIE shows MOTHER the photograph of her sister. GHOST enters with a framed picture of herself as a little girl. She moves toward SOPHIE.*

MOTHER You from around here?

SOPHIE Yeah.

MOTHER You went to the States after the war?

SOPHIE Right.

> *DAUGHTER goes to pool and down on her knees. She*

bathes her face with water. GHOST stops moving.

DAUGHTER When the war started, the black dog soldiers wanted to kill us, but it rained a lot and the river got higher, and higher, and they couldn't kill us in the big field because the river had flooded and they didn't have any boats that could get us. But those black dog soldiers still got the people like catching frogs in a swamp. They pile them up, wash them, take their souls out like empty cans, and burn them by the river at night. The smoke drips and moans as rises, and covers the stars so you can't hear them. The next morning, it was still dark - you couldn't see the sun for three years - from 1975 to 1978, there was no sun around here. You couldn't see, nothing grew and you couldn't play. Only, burning, darkness, and people crying for water.

> *DAUGHTER grins and smiles broadly. SOPHIE stares at her. GHOST sits at SOPHIE'S feet with the picture as MOTHER hands the photograph back to SOPHIE.*

MOTHER I haven't seen her.

DAUGHTER Looks kinda like me. Pretty.

MOTHER No it doesn't! I'm sorry, but I can't help you.

SOPHIE Are you sure?

MOTHER There are other people who might be able to help you find her. I could see about that if you want.

> *GUARD enters dressed in khaki pants and a plain white shirt. Background Cambodian romantic pop music cuts to uptempo, jaunty, groovy, Cambodian era-specific male vocal dance rock music.*

GUARD Hello! Perhaps I could help you.

SOPHIE Hi.

GUARD How are you?

SOPHIE Fine.

GUARD Beautiful day.

SOPHIE Yeah.

GUARD Very beautiful temples.

SOPHIE I dig it.

GUARD Right... so what're you doing in the temples today?

DAUGHTER *(tugging on his arm)* Looking for water. Have you got any?

GUARD No, I haven't. When're you gonna take your daughter to the hospital?

MOTHER *(pulling DAUGHTER back)* She doesn't need to go to the hospital.

GUARD Where you from?

SOPHIE America.

GUARD Oh... how big's your airplane?

SOPHIE Which one?

GUARD What do you uh... think of our temples?

SOPHIE Awesome.

GUARD Of course. There's temples all over the place. Beautiful temples. They're the pride of our country. Built 800 years ago by the ancient kings. The symbols of our countries past glory and the hopes of our nation's prosperous future. These, are the most famous, the best temples in the world.

SOPHIE I know.

GUARD You do?

SOPHIE Yeah man.

MOTHER She's a local girl. Went to the States after the war.

GUARD Really? You don't look like one of our girls to me. You look like a foreigner. *(laughs)*

SOPHIE I got my own style, ya know what I'm sayin'?

GUARD I'm sorry, pardon me.

MOTHER Everything's real different in America. They've got some things you never heard of. "Electric can openers."

GUARD Really? Hmm. Sounds like America. So why'd you come back?

SOPHIE To look for my sister. I really don't know if she's alive or dead. Have you ever seen this girl?

> *Music reverts to moody, deep male-vocal Cambodian folk music in background.*
>
> *SOPHIE shows GUARD the photo of her sister. GHOST balances her picture in the pool and bathes her face with the pool water.*

DAUGHTER When the darkness left, the people stopped crying, and then they ran to the river. After they went looking for their relatives. They looked and looked all over the place. But all they found was... old pictures. Old pictures stuck in the mud, buried under the leaves. In the fields, in the ditches, lying on the road in town. Sometimes... pictures under water. After they picked up the pictures, flowers and babies grew right where they picked 'em up! *(Smiles broadly)*

GUARD When was the last time you saw your sister?

> *During this next speech, GHOST "washes" picture and leaves it standing in the pool; then slowly exits upstage arch.*

SOPHIE My whole family was going to the border. We split up so the soldiers wouldn't find all of us together. I was with my sister, and we were supposed to meet our dad on the other side. But my sister hurt her leg, and I went to go find our dad. That was the last time I saw her.

GUARD *(giving photo back)* What would you say if I said I saw her?

SOPHIE That would be cool.

GUARD I think I've seen her.

SOPHIE Yeah! Great! Where?

GUARD In the prison at the army base.

SOPHIE *(pause)* Why would she be there?

GUARD *(pause)* She must have gotten arrested.

SOPHIE *(pause)* Arrested for what?

GUARD I don't know. Who knows. Could be one of many things.

> *Pause.*

Maybe... she was arrested for being a spy.

SOPHIE A spy? Why would they think that?

GUARD Maybe she did something. Maybe she was trying to sneak out of the country.

SOPHIE Is she still there?

GUARD I heard a rumor that she escaped. But there's lots of rumors around here. I also heard a rumor that ...

> *GUARD mimes shooting a machine gun. SOPHIE starts to leave.*

GUARD Where you going?

SOPHIE I gotta go down there and ask about her.

GUARD I wouldn't do that if I were you.

SOPHIE Why not?

GUARD Well, since you're related to her, they might come to the same conclusion about you.

SOPHIE Like what?

GUARD Like you're a spy.

SOPHIE *(pause)* A spy.

GUARD *(pauses and smiles)* A spy.

> *BLINDFOLDED GHOST, dressed like GHOST, appears in the upper archway holding a large bouquet of flowers, and stands in the doorway.*

GUARD Interesting story. Left after the war. Went to America, which bombed us. and now you come back, looking for your sister, who was arrested for being a spy? You didn't come back just to look for your sister. You came back for another reason. To spy on us. And go back and report to the Americans what you saw. Our economy. Our army. Our infrastructure.

SOPHIE That's crazy.

GUARD We can't trust you.

SOPHIE Why not.

GUARD You have to watch out for people who are different, especially for foreigners. People who are different don't think the same as you do. They can misunderstand you, make mistakes about you and cause you a lotta trouble.

SOPHIE I dunno what you're talking about.

GUARD Sure you do. We hear there's many kinds of Americans. Whites, blacks, everybody. Do you trust them? Do you trust all the people on the streets of your country?

SOPHIE Well, not really, but...

GUARD Exactly what I thought! And how do you make that judgment? You make that judgment based on their appearance, the way they look and where they're from. Right? Don't think we're so stupid. People are the same the world over. Everybody's afraid to trust the unknown. It's dangerous. It's normal. You're not a local girl anymore. I can't afford to allow you to be trusted by the local population. They could be swayed by you, unduly influenced. If you're innocent, of course, the police will let you go. I'm taking you into custody to protect civil order.

GUARD reaches to grab SOPHIE's arm.

SOPHIE *(striking martial arts position)* No you're not!

GUARD So... you know how to fight?

SOPHIE Yeah man. Come on.

GUARD We'll see about this. I'll go and get help. The police.

GUARD exits. SOPHIE moves to leave after seeing that he's gone and the coast is clear, but MOTHER reaches in her bag and pulls out AK-47 machine gun.

MOTHER Just stay right there.

SOPHIE Shit!

As MOTHER motions for SOPHIE to move to center stage and sit down, GHOST enters. She carries a bundle of large pictures. Over the next scene, GHOST and BLINDFOLDED GHOST slowly set up all the pictures in a loose line across the upstage area; the pictures, large scale old portraits of anonymous people, young and old, male and female, are set out face forward, standing up. BLINDFOLDED GHOST sets a flower at the base of each photo.

SOPHIE Listen, my sister's normal. I'm sure she hasn't done anything.

MOTHER It's not her we're worried about.

SOPHIE I'm from here. I remember everything. I remember the food, the people. I remember the city people, the way they are, and the farmers, the way you are. We're the same people.

Folk music fades out leaving only jungle soundscape.

MOTHER Doesn't look like it to me. Look at my daughter. You're only a little older than she is, and you're not like her at all. Look what the war did to her. She's a lunatic.

DAUGHTER strokes water in pool with her hand.

DAUGHTER People afraid of old pictures. When old picture comes out of a hole in the ground, it's burning hot metal. It burns a hole in people's memories, and lets all that stuff trapped in there out. Like... the rice warehouse empty, not even one grain, but a million butterflies panting in the shadows. The wrecked temple with a yucky pond. Dresses and shirts laid out on the roads everywhere, clean and pressed, with the person's name written on the lapel of each one. They lie there on the roads for years, burning in the hot sun, the names fading. People afraid of old pictures, they want to bury them, in a garden, in a field, or under a building.

SOPHIE I'm sorry. But a lot of stuff happened to my family too, ya know.

MOTHER Like what?

SOPHIE *(pause)* We walked a long time - saw a lot of dead people - we were so thirsty we drank cow's blood. It was so hot, we were baking like an oven, my skin started peeling, I thought I was gonna die - but I was just a kid, I thought dying was just sleeping a long time - so I was so tired I wanted to "die" too. I wanted to count the dead people, but I hadn't gone to school yet, so I couldn't count very high.

MOTHER Your story's everybody's story. It's the whole country's. When those black dogs got all the people down by the river, it was everybody - the farmer, the bus driver, the student. When they forced people to pull the plow like a cow, it was everybody - the teacher, the policeman, the musician, the criminal. *(jungle soundscape fades out)* When they went to the mountains, everybody cried - the businessman, the beggar, the cripple. When people went looking for their family, it was everybody -the monk, the fish seller, the gas station attendant. And everything that happened to everybody else happened to me and my daughter too. We were forced to leave our home and sleep in the forest. Everybody I knew was forced to go somewhere else, I never saw them again. Only my daughter came back, and she came back like this. When the black dogs came, they tore up the calendars to roll cigarettes, so I have no idea how long this went on. Other people would try to count the days, the months, the years, as a way to remember. Not me. I have no idea how long all that went on. I'm glad about that. I don't wanna know.

DAUGHTER People afraid of the past - have stopped looking for somebody. A person passes away - smoke goes through an open window in a building in the city.

> *A clock projection appears on the temple face upstage, as stage lights dim.*

DAUGHTER Outside the window, there's a clock on the wall. Smoke goes through the open window, and the clock goes tick, tick, tick. All that's left of the person is a picture. The picture falls on the ground, onto a pile of more pictures. Smoke goes through the window, and the clock goes tick, tick, tick.

> *Clock projection fades out, and stage lights return to previous setting.*
>
> *Having finished setting out all the pictures upstage, GHOST and BLINDFOLDED GHOST sit together and listen to SOPHIE and the others. Jungle soundscape fades in again.*

MOTHER I live for her. I'm so happy she survived. Maybe you can be happy with the way things are, instead of trying to make things be the way you want them to be.

SOPHIE Well I'm happy with the way I am, instead of the way I want things to be.

MOTHER And how are you?

SOPHIE I'm Chinese Cambodian American.

MOTHER Chinese Cambodian Am...? *(laughs)* If there's any Cambodian part to you anymore, I can't see it. You've moved around so much, you've changed. You're different. You're not one of us. You never should've left.

> *GHOST slowly holds mirror up to SOPHIE.*

SOPHIE Listen to me. Listen to me! My family's from up north. They came down here 50 years ago. They settled in the next town. I was born in the hospital there, I lived there as a little girl, and I was just like everybody else. After the war, we went to America to get away from the killing. That's the only reason. And if you stay in America a while, you can become an American citizen. I have Chinese blood, a Cambodian past, and an American passport. I'm Chinese Cambodian American. I'm all three - in one.

MOTHER So where's your home? Do you feel at home in the States?

SOPHIE Sometimes.

MOTHER Sometimes?

SOPHIE It's hard to explain. Everybody in America's from somewhere else. Immigrants from all over the world. And I'm the newest one. Some who've been there longer than me treat me like I don't belong there. Like I'm an outsider. Like I'm inferior cuz I'm different. I am different - but I'm the same. I'm part of the group - but I'm different. I'm a foreigner and a homegirl. I'm stuck - but I'm proud of who I am. I don't need a reason. I just am.

> *GUARD returns. GHOST puts down mirror and listens to the others.*

MOTHER Where's the police?

GUARD The road's blocked.

MOTHER Whaddaya mean?

GUARD The black dogs have blocked the road. We can't get out.

> *Mortar shell explodes nearby followed by occasional small arms fire heard in the background.*

DAUGHTER What're we gonna do, mama?

GUARD I bet she has something to do with it. Did you hear that noise? It's an assault. Heading this way.

> *Another shell and explosions seem louder.*

MOTHER *(to SOPHIE)* There's land mines all around the temple. It would be suicide to go overland. The road's the only way out.

GUARD We should give up. We don't have any guns.

MOTHER *(points her weapon at GUARD)* I gotta gun.

GUARD What're you doing?

MOTHER You want us to give up so they'll get us. You made some kinda deal with them.

GUARD You're crazy.

MOTHER You're always pushing us around.

GUARD I should've kept an eye on you from the beginning. I've suspected you from the start.

MOTHER Of what?

GUARD Where'd you get that gun anyway?

MOTHER Don't treat me like a child! Everybody knows where to get guns. You get guns from the market. And the market gets them from government guys like you. If you weren't so corrupt, we could've stopped the black dogs and not had to live three years without sunshine.

> *A close shell causes them all to flinch. Attack sounds increase in intensity.*

GUARD So what're you gonna do? Shoot me? Shoot us all! Shoot yourself if you're so unhappy!

> *DAUGHTER takes the gun from MOTHER.*

DAUGHTER Stay away from my mother!

GUARD The idiot has it!

> *DAUGHTER points the gun in the general direction of GUARD and SOPHIE. They dive to the ground. She pulls the trigger, and the gun clicks audibly without firing.*

DAUGHTER Hmm. Broken.

SOPHIE *(jumps up)* Son of a bitch! FUCK THIS SHIT!

> *SOPHIE grabs gun and flings it offstage. Small explosion is heard offstage in that direction.*

SOPHIE I oughta take ya off the planet, bitch!

> *GHOST and BLINDFOLDED GHOST exit.*

GUARD What're we gonna do?

DAUGHTER When the black dogs went to eat all the froggies, the smart froggie played dead.

SOPHIE Hey. Right on. You're not as crazy as I thought you were. We'll play dead.

GUARD What?

SOPHIE We'll act like we're dead up here. Maybe they won't find us. It's our only chance.

GUARD I think you're setting up a trap. Maybe you know the black dogs. You collude with them. She's carrying around a picture of a spy, she's probably a spy herself.

SOPHIE Listen, I DON'T GIVE A FUCK IF YOU THINK I'M AN AMERICAN, A FOREIGNER, OR WHAT. BUT THAT'S A PICTURE OF MY SISTER, MY PAST, MY FAMILY, AND YOU DON'T DISS MY SISTER! She's not a spy, I'm not a spy, nobody's a spy, motherfucker! I'm just a person tryin' to live, just a fuckin' person, ya know what I'm saying'?

GUARD I saw the black dogs wreck our country. They pushed my whole family out into the mountains. I was always working like a slave, running to hide, or eating leaves. I walked all the way across the country by myself, and I was just a kid. I didn't get to grow up slow, I had to grow up fast. I hate my country! I hate my home! All I wanna do is forget it. That's how I wanna live.

SOPHIE What kinda life is that?

MOTHER They're getting closer.

SOPHIE We're gonna hide together. If we split up, we could go one by one. I've been through stuff like this, and we'll be OK, no matter what you think of me. We're gonna hide, nobody's gonna make a sound, and we're gonna get through this together, right?

DAUGHTER *(looking at pool of water)* Before the war,

everybody trust everybody in our country. You need food, people give you food. You hurt, people put out your fire. You lost at night, a man's head is a flashlight, he shines on the road for you to find your house. But then the black dogs came. Nothing ever the same.

All go hide under temple head in the archway.

Explosions end and sound piece ends.

BLACK DOG SOLDIER creeps on wearing a dog helmet-mask, somewhat like a hat, which partially obscures his face; a black outfit with sandals, a faded red scarf, a large, tripod machine gun over his shoulder, and carries two large, worn canvas bags. He looks around stealthily to see that he is alone, then falls to his knees.

Heavy melancholic Cambodian male vocal song comes up.

BLACK DOG SOLDIER opens the first bag and takes out a large, poster-sized faded color photograph of a man in a military uniform with skulls garlanding the edge frame. The photo is of Pol Pot. BLACK DOG SOLDIER places the picture up center stage, and, on knees, reverently bows three times to it in traditional Cambodian fashion.

BLACK DOG SOLDIER opens the second bag near the pool and begins to carefully pull many skulls out of the bag, and places them on the ground. He cherishes them. Then he dips his finger into the water and tastes it.

DAUGHTER comes out from the archway. BLACK DOG SOLDIER senses her movement and stops, noticing. SOPHIE comes out and, grabbing DAUGHTER'S arm, pulls her back and they disappear under the archway.

Cambodian song fades out.

BLACK DOG SOLDIER rises, takes the picture of Pol

Pot and, holding it high in the air in hero worship, ritualistically exits.

DAUGHTER enters from upstage and slowly walks to pool area, surveying skulls. Then she kneels by the pool.

A gentle, circular, repetitive, gorgeous atmospheric Cambodian instrumental music begins.

DAUGHTER takes a single skull into her hands, gently washes it in the pool, and sets the skull down upstage of the pool, upright on the ground. She washes another skull, and continues washing the skulls and creates a short pyramid pile of them. SOPHIE enters and helps DAUGHTER with the final skulls, creating a pyramid of skulls above the pool. Having finished creating the skull pyramid, DAUGHTER sits behind it.

GHOST and BLINDFOLDED GHOST, still with flowers, enter, and as GHOST sits to the left of the skull pile, BLINDFOLDED GHOST places half the flowers on the left side of the skull pile, and then the other half on the right side of the pile, then he sits on the right side.

Music fades out.

DAUGHTER Help the dead to rest. Remember what the black dogs did to them.

SOPHIE I remember them.

GUARD and MOTHER enter.

GUARD When you see those black dogs coming, you know you're in for trouble.

SOPHIE I've seen them before. What're they doing?

MOTHER Trying to hide what they did. They hope

everybody'll forget.

SOPHIE If everybody forgets... who'll stop them?

GUARD It's easy to forget. Harder to remember.

DAUGHTER Mama... I wanna go home.

MOTHER We gotta go.

MOTHER gathers up things.

GUARD I'd better continue on my rounds. I'll file a report at the central station about what happened. I'm glad nobody got hurt. So when're you going back to the States?

SOPHIE I dunno.

GUARD Are you still gonna look for your sister?

SOPHIE Yeah.

GUARD What're you gonna tell everybody if you can't find her?

SOPHIE If I don't find her, I'll just keep looking. And I'll tell everybody that we have to trust that she's alive and OK. We can't forget her. And we can't forget that the black dogs are still around, and that they haven't changed. They hope everybody'll forget. I won't. I won't forget anything. I owe it to my sister, I owe it to my country, and I owe it - to everybody.

GUARD What if she's dead?

SOPHIE Then I'll never stop looking, will I?

GUARD Good luck.

GUARD reaches out to shake SOPHIE'S hand - she

reluctantly shakes.

MOTHER Show the picture to other people. You'll find her. You must really love your sister. You're a good girl. Please forgive me.

DAUGHTER Trust that she's alive and OK. Find all the pictures, clean them, take care of them, and don't leave them in the yucky mucky. Remember the pictures and keep them together, cuz the pictures can live if you trust them, and if they get forgotten in the yucky, the black dogs will burn the people again. And if the black dogs try to burn the people again, if the people all stay together he can't burn them all at the same time just like when he tries to eat a whole mouthful of froggies he can't cuz his mouth's too full he has too many so he has to spit them all out, and they can all run away and hide back in the swamp!

DAUGHTER jumps up and down with excitement.

SOPHIE Girl, you be trippin'.

DAUGHTER *(smiling broadly)* When you get back to America, can you send my mother the electric can opener?

SOPHIE Better yet, I'll bring one the next time I fly this way.

GUARD Thank you again.

MOTHER Good bye.

> *DAUGHTER bows to SOPHIE in Cambodian style.*
> *SOPHIE takes off an earring and gives it to DAUGHTER.*
> *DAUGHTER goes to the pool and puts water on her face.*

DAUGHTER Trust the pictures, search for them... search again... and again.

Uptempo, loud, stirring Cambodian female-vocal dance

rock starts.

*GUARD, MOTHER and DAUGHTER exit. SOPHIE
gazes at them as they disappear into the distance. GHOST
and BLINDFOLDED GHOST rise and bow to each other
in Cambodian sompeah style. BLINDFOLDED GHOST
exits through archway.*

*SOPHIE goes to the goddess statue and picks up the small
mirror. She goes center stage and gazes at herself in the
mirror.*

*GHOST sits at SOPHIE'S feet and, leaning against her,
begins gently combing her own hair. SOPHIE takes
Raiders cap off, and hand with mirror also comes down.
SOPHIE turns to gaze at upstage head, then ritualistically
walks through the archway, disappearing into the back.
GHOST continues to comb her hair as lights and music
ever so gently fade out, as lights and music hit blackout on
final note of song.*

FINI

About the Author

Mark Knego hails from Napa, California, where he lived with his parents, George and Barbara Knego, and his three brothers. Being in a military family, he travelled much as a youth, and gained a lifelong love of travelling. Mark attended the University of California at Davis from 1972-76 and graduated with a Bachelor of Arts degree in Dramatic Art. At UC Davis, in addition to having the benefit of a great program with a terrific faculty and staff, he was able to meet Peter Schumann of the Bread and Puppet Theater. For the following two summers, he worked with the Bread and Puppet Theater at their farm in Glover, Vermont on their annual show, Our Domestic Resurrection Circus. This experience impressed the universality and expression inherent in mask art on him deeply.

From 1980-82 Mark lived in Florence, Italy and formed Dream Theater with his lifelong friend Jeff Gere; and toured Germany in June, 1982. Upon returning to San Francisco, Mark began teaching mask making at various venues, and writing, producing and performing in his own pieces, most notably 1984's "Future Junkyard". He also began to market animal sculptures in paper-mache through various galleries, most notably the Virginia Breier Gallery in San Francisco; and including galleries and venues in Santa Monica, Los Angeles, Cambridge, Mexico City and others. His work is included in the collections of personages such as Thomas Peters, Richard Crenna and Robin Williams.

In 1987 he received a California Arts Council Artist-in-Residence grant, charged to provide art instruction and practice to underserved communities. These communities were targeted in the Tenderloin and the South of Market areas in San Francisco. Sponsored by SOMAR, South of Market Art Resources, Mark retained a studio and conducted art classes in "Mask Making as an Art Form" at SOMAR from 1987-2001, serving hundreds of students and fellow artists. He also taught at North of Market Senior Services, the Tenderloin Reflection and Education Center

(TREC), and many other venues.

His Cambodia Trilogy was developed with EXIT Theatre, with *Snakes of Kampuchea* premiering in 1991, *Tual Kan's Journey* in 1993 and *Return to Angkor* in 1994. Mark also did volunteer and commission work for numerous other Bay Area theater groups, including Snake Theater, Nightletter Theater, the San Francisco Mime Troupe and others.

Through the late 1990's Marks' sculpture work also encompassed plaster and he created the "Fashion Model" series.

In recent years Mark's artistic interests have evolved into short films, video and photography. He has shown his films at his favorite San Francisco theater, EXIT Theatre. He has been lucky to travel to distant countries such as Pakistan, India, Uzbekistan, Japan, Honduras and many others. He's working on a long term photo project, a photobook tentatively titled "Whispers from within the Firmament of Globalization".

Mark digs melodic music and Tibetan Buddhism. Believing himself to be a reincarnated fat cat, he enjoys lolling in the sun on a beautiful day.

EXIT Press

EXIT Press is the publishing division of EXIT Theatre, a San Francisco theater company that was founded in 1983. Published books include *Ten Plays* by Mark Jackson and *Snakes of Kampuchea* by Mark Knego. Coming soon are translations of *Woyzeck*, *Pelleas and Melisande* and *Ubu Roi* by Rob Melrose and *Practical Tales For Children and other stories* by Mark Romyn.

May 2011

www.ingramcontent.com/pod-product-compliance
Lightning Source LLC
La Vergne TN
LVHW091310080426
835510LV00007B/449